HARRINGTON AND HIS *OCEANA*

HARRINGTON

AND HIS

OCEANA

A STUDY OF A 17TH CENTURY UTOPIA
AND ITS INFLUENCE IN AMERICA

BY

H. F. RUSSELL SMITH, M.A.

1971

OCTAGON BOOKS
New York

First published 1914

Reprinted 1971
by permission of Cambridge University Press

OCTAGON BOOKS
A DIVISION OF FARRAR, STRAUS & GIROUX, INC.
19 Union Square West
New York, N. Y. 10003

LIBRARY OF CONGRESS CATALOG CARD NUMBER: 70-159228

ISBN 0-374-96996-5

Printed in U.S.A. by
NOBLE OFFSET PRINTERS, INC.
NEW YORK 3, N. Y.

PREFACE

MY attention was drawn to the ideas of Harrington when I was studying the history of toleration in the Stuart period. It appeared to me that his influence in England and in her colonies, both at his own time and since, deserved a fuller examination than it had yet received. My tenure of the Allen Scholarship in 1911 enabled me to make some researches both in England and America, which I have brought together in the following essay. I have attempted in the first place to give some account of Harrington's political ideas, describing their origin, their history, and their subsequent influence on two centuries of English political thought ; in the second place, to trace a connection, which has often been surmised but never established, between *Oceana* and the political institutions of America ; and finally to discuss the revival of Harrington's chief theories in the constitutions of revolutionary France. In this way I hope incidentally to have given a new illustration of the connection between political theory and practice, and to have shown afresh the essential unity of the three great revolutions of modern Europe.

The authorities for a study like this are necessarily various, but they are for the most part readily accessible. The history of Harrington's public life is drawn largely from the Thomason Pamphlets in the British Museum. The contention that Grote's advocacy of the ballot was due to his study of Harrington rests on Grote's unpublished essay on *Oceana,*

also in the British Museum. The most important
evidence for establishing Harrington's influence in
Pennsylvania is supplied by the preliminary drafts
of the first constitution of Pennsylvania, which exist
in manuscript in the possession of the Pennsylvania
Historical Society.

Of secondary authorities little more need be
said. There have not been many recent notices of
Harrington's work. The article in the *English
Historical Review* (April 1891), and the chapter on
Harrington in Franck's *Reformateurs et Publicistes
de l'Europe* are nothing but summaries of *Oceana*.
The article by Theodore Dwight in the *Political
Science Quarterly* (March 1887) is more valuable,
being written partly from the American point of view.
The best accounts are to be found in Masson's *Life
of Milton*, Prof. C. H. Firth's *Last Years of the
Protectorate*, and in Mr G. P. Gooch's *History of
Democratic Ideas in the Seventeenth Century*, to all of
which I am much indebted. I had concluded that
there must have been some connection between Penn
and Harrington before I discovered that the same
idea had occurred to Dr W. R. Shepherd, the author
of *Pennsylvania as a Proprietary Colony*. I had
studied the influence of Harrington on Sieyès before
the appearance of Mr J. H. Clapham's recent book,
The Abbé Sieyès, from which I have, however,
borrowed one valuable reference. The fact that these
connections have been seen by writers who can be
said to have no prejudices in the matter seems to me
to lend additional support to a contention which
might appear to be due to bias, when made in an
essay written for the purpose of tracing Harrington's
influence.

Of the editions of Harrington's works something

is said in the text.   For the present work I have made use of Toland's edition of Harrington's *Works*, 1747 (the 3rd edition), giving the name of the particular writing to which I have referred and the page on which my reference is to be found in the collected *Works*.

It is my pleasant duty to acknowledge the courtesy and kindness which were shown me while I was carrying on my investigations in America by scholars too numerous to mention ; and to thank Professor Firth for valuable suggestions in regard to the first four chapters, and Mr E. A. Benians of my own college for reading this essay both in manuscript and proof, and assisting me throughout by his sympathetic criticism.

H. F. R. S.

St John's College
Cambridge, *March* 1914

CONTENTS

CHAPTER I

THE AUTHOR OF *OCEANA*

CHAPTER II

THE FORM AND METHOD OF *OCEANA*

CHAPTER III

THE POLITICAL IDEAS OF *OCEANA*

CHAPTER IV

HARRINGTON'S PUBLIC LIFE AND MINOR WRITINGS

CHAPTER V

CONTEMPORARY CRITICISM OF HARRINGTON'S THEORIES

CHAPTER VI

HARRINGTON'S LAST YEARS. HIS SUBSEQUENT INFLUENCE IN ENGLAND

CHAPTER VII

HARRINGTON'S INFLUENCE IN AMERICA DURING THE SEVENTEENTH CENTURY

CHAPTER VIII

HARRINGTON'S INFLUENCE ON THE AMERICAN REVOLUTION

CHAPTER IX

HARRINGTON'S INFLUENCE IN FRANCE

CHAPTER I

IN those critical years of dispute between James I. and his parliaments, when the Tudor system of government was on the eve of collapse, history records the birth of the strange writer, who was afterwards to give a logical explanation of the collapse and to suggest to deaf ears a way by which republicanism might avoid the same catastrophe.

Like many of the opponents of the Stuart régime, James Harrington came of a good family, and a family that took pride in its greatness. He could trace his ancestry back to the twelfth century, when a younger branch of the family, at that time influential in Cumberland, came by marriage into possession of the property belonging to Exton House, Exton, Rutlandshire. Several members of the family achieved fame. Sir John Harrington, created Baron Harrington of Exton in 1603, was a well-known figure in his time. He was selected for his piety and learning to be tutor to the King's daughter, Elizabeth, who afterwards married the Elector Palatine and became the unhappy Winter Queen of Bohemia. His son, a traveller and an accomplished linguist, was Prince Henry's favourite companion; and his premature death was mourned like the death of Germanicus. Sir John Harrington, the poet, was the first baron's cousin. His father had been one of Henry VIII.'s confidential advisers. He himself, with Queen Elizabeth as his godmother, played a prominent part in the life of the

Court, combining the parts of poet, wit, and scholar with considerable success. His reputation was such that the royal servants were compelled to lavish every attention on him from fear of the epigrams with which their shortcomings used to be accompanied. His writings were amorous and sometimes indecent, so that he earned from the Queen the title " saucy poet," but at the same time he was able to study the religious questions of the day, and he actually proposed himself as successor to Archbishop Loftus in the Irish see.

The Harringtons were an interesting family with qualities which would win them a place in seventeenth-century society. They had travelled on the continent. They were linguists, scholars, and gentlemen. They were at the same time men of character and men of charm.

Some painstaking chronologist of the time of James II. calculated that no fewer than eight dukes, three marquises, seventy earls, nine counts, twenty-seven viscounts, and thirty-six barons (sixteen out of this total having been made Knights of the Garter) were descendants or nearly allied to the descendants of the baron's father, Sir James Harrington.[1] James Harrington himself, in whom we shall see many of the family characteristics, was a great-nephew of the first Lord Harrington, being the eldest son of Sir Sapcote Harrington and Jane, daughter of Sir William Samuel of Upton in Northamptonshire. He was born on Friday, January 3rd, 1611, at the seat of his mother's family.

Of his youth little is known. He was one of eight children, and appears to have been somewhat precocious. His sister, to whom we are indirectly in-

[1] Wright, " History and Antiquities of Rutlandshire," p. 52.

debted for much that we know of his life, remembered him as a boy of a grave disposition with a keen desire for knowledge, who rather frightened his parents with his learning.[1] He entered Trinity College, Oxford, in 1629, as a gentleman commoner, under the famous rational theologian Chillingworth, whose influence we may perhaps see in Harrington's views of religious liberty. After devoting himself to a study of modern as well as of ancient languages, he left the University without taking a degree. He was admitted to the Middle Temple in 1631.[2]

The next stage in his education was the one to which he himself attached the greatest importance—travel. The continent was visited in the seventeenth century by a large number of Englishmen, of whom some went to fight, some to avoid persecution, some to study ; others mainly to gain the experience and educational advantages of travel. Those who were in search of employment as soldiers and those who wanted religious liberty generally went to the Netherlands ; students and travellers made their way to Italy, and often came back with a new and wider outlook. This intellectual development, which can be seen in varying degrees in men like Pym, Hampden, Sidney, Penn, Locke, Nevile, Marvell, and Milton—all of whom visited the continent, is unmistakable in the case of Harrington.

Harrington spent the first part of his time in the Netherlands, where he enlisted under the Earl of Craven, in an English volunteer regiment. He was thus brought into contact with the court of the Prince of Orange, as well as that of his great-uncle's pupil, now

---

[1] The life of Harrington by Toland, prefixed to his collection of Harrington's Works, was compiled chiefly from material supplied by the Lady Ashton, his eldest sister.

[2] "Middle Temple Records," ii. 784.

wife of the unfortunate exile from the Palatinate.   He
soon became a great favourite with Frederick's family,
and later we find him trying to repay the kindness
which they showed him, by appealing to the Commons
to help them in their misfortunes.[1]   With Frederick
he went for a time to the Court of Denmark.   On his
return he left his position at the Hague, and with a
view to completing his education, moved on through
Flanders and France to Italy.   We know little of his
travels, except that he learned the languages of the
countries he visited, and made careful observations of
their political and social institutions.   Isolated stories
have been preserved to the effect that he refused to
kiss the Pope's toe, and expressed disbelief in contemporary Italian miracles.   But that is all.   After a stay
at Venice, which made a profound impression on him
—not by the beauty of its canals, but by the beauty
of its constitution—he came home through the west
of Germany

The exact date of his return to England is not
known.   At any rate he was back before the outbreak
of the Civil War, equipped with a peculiar training.
He had received hospitality from monarchs.   He had
travelled over the continent at the time of the great
unrest and disorder, which spread over the whole of
western Europe in the train of the Thirty Years' War.
He had witnessed something of the great religious
struggles, which seemed to him to cast so deep a stain
on the name of religion ; he had visited the Holy See
and seen the holder of the office which he accounted
solely responsible for this degradation of Christianity ; [2]
he had found one little bright spot in a world of chaos—

[1] Hist. MSS. Commission, XIII. i. 210.
[2] " Oceana," p. 59. References are to the third edition of his collected
Works (1747).

an island city with a sense of order and permanence about it. The Netherlands and Venice alike captivated his imagination and roused his enthusiasm, but in a rather different way. In the Netherlands he had seen what a people can do. In Venice he was shown what institutions can achieve. The former turned his interests in the direction of politics ; [1] the latter made him believe in political science. With his faith in the people and his faith in institutions his mind was moving in the direction of republicanism.

Having assisted in settling the future of his brothers and sisters, who were now growing up and had been left fatherless, while their elder brother was at Oxford, Harrington had his own problem to decide. His interests were political, and it was apparent that he must play a part either as actor or student in the world of politics. The rapid march of events and the growing breach between King and Parliament necessitated some decision, if only a decision to remain neutral. The choice of sides, which troubled many minds at the beginning of the Civil War in England, must have been peculiarly difficult for one whose traditional connection with the court was counterbalanced by a theoretical admiration of continental republicanism. It is therefore not surprising that after having accompanied his Majesty to Scotland in the first Bishops' War (1639) as a member of the Privy Chamber Extraordinary, Harrington retired from activity till the fighting was over.[2] It is true that he is reported to have attempted to enter Parliament in 1642,[3] but it was not till January 1647 that he came before the public eye, when hoping to use his influence with Charles to bring about a settlement he attached himself to the Commissioners

---

[1] Toland's Introduction, xiv.　　　　　　　　　　　[2] *Ibid.* xv.
[3] Wood, " Athenæ Oxonienses," iii. 1115.

of the Parliament, who were sent to treat with the King at Newcastle.[1]   He remained with his Majesty until May, and he was then appointed, with Thomas Herbert, Groom of the Bedchamber.   He was the obvious man for the post, being in sympathy with the parliamentary party, but liked by the King ; and he had moved in continental courts.   He was with Charles during his stay at Holmby House, and went with him to Carisbrooke Castle and then to Hurst Castle.   Here he offended the Governor and some Roundhead officers by what was a very moderate defence of the King's attitude with regard to the Treaty of Newport and the proposal for the establishment of Presbyterianism in England, and was dismissed from his post.[2]   On Charles's removal to Windsor he was permitted to return for three or four days, but was again dismissed for refusing to swear not to assist in any attempt to procure his Majesty's escape.[3]   He was imprisoned for a short time for his obstinacy, but he managed to see his beloved King once again before his death, received a present from him, and witnessed the execution.

This affection between one of the most determined, if not one of the greatest, of the republicans of the time and the sovereign who has enchanted half posterity by his kingliness is not a little remarkable.   But both were men who could admire the personal qualities of their friends, however much they disagreed on questions of politics.   Harrington was a good example of an English gentleman.   He is described as a man

---

[1] Wood, "Athenæ Oxonienses," iii. 1115, and Herbert, " Memoirs of the Two Last Years of the Reign of . . . King Charles I.," p. 7.

[2] *Ibid.* iii. 1116 ; Herbert, p. 90.

[3] Toland, xvii., and " Kingdom's Moderate Intelligencer " of Jan. 2, 1649. If we follow Toland and accept two dismissals of Harrington, the difficulty which Gardiner sees (*vide* " Civil War," iii. 548, note) disappears.

" of a middling stature, a well trussed man, strong and thick, well sett, sanguine, quick—hott—fiery hazell eie, thick moyst curled hair " ;[1] a man " of a very liberal and compassionate nature " ;[2] " in his conversation very friendly and facetious and hospitable."[3] He was adored by his family ; he was beloved by various friends, to whom he gave financial support as well as friendship ; he delighted the young princesses at the Hague by his grace ; he found a place in the heart of the King. Aubrey, who was one of Harrington's greatest friends, alluding to the political discourses with which Harrington entertained the King during this unhappy period, bears witness how " the King loved his company ; only he would not endure to heare of a Commonwealth ; and Mr Harrington passionately loved his Majestie " ; and he says further that Harrington was so much distressed by the death of the King that he " contracted a disease by it."[4] But he was not shaken in his republican principles by the charms of one that bore the name of King.

While England was making her first experiments in republican government, her republican philosopher remained in retirement. He was studying ancient history and continuing the collection of political writings, which he had started at Venice, preparing for future fame. One of his hobbies during this period was a translation of Vergil. He was no poet, as his friend Nevile, the author of " Plato Redivivus " and the leader of Harrington's party in the parliament of 1659, wisely told him.[5] But he was inspired by the examples of the statesmen he admired—Moses, Lycurgus, Machiavelli

[1] Aubrey, " Brief Lives," i. 293.
[2] Toland, xvi.
[3] Aubrey, i. 293.
[4] *Ibid*. i. 288-89.
[5] *Ibid*. i. 289.

—to try his hand at versification, and he produced translations of certain Vergilian eclogues and the first six books of the " Æneid," which were published in 1658 and 1659.[1] The translations are not very successful. They are not without interest as early specimens of English renderings of Vergil, but their chief importance lies in the light which they throw on the nature of Harrington's mind ; for they show an artistic sense, subservient always to the artist's interest in politics. In his rendering of the " Eclogues " he could not refrain from introducing his pet theory of the " balance or property," first as a note explaining the fall of the Roman Empire, then as an ode to the theory which could explain it,[2] while in his translation of the " Æneid " he did not hesitate to distort a passage in the fourth book so as to introduce the same theory into the text itself.[3] But translating Vergil was only a hobby. The real work in which he was engaged during the seven years which succeeded the execution of the King was preparation for the composition of " Oceana." The book which was to win him fame was written in response to a request for some public protest against the Instrument of Government. A fairly persistent rumour credited Nevile with a share

---

[1] " An Essay upon two of Virgil's Eclogues and two books of his Æneid," 1658, and " Virgil's Æneid, the Third, Fourth, Fifth and Sixth Books." James Harrington, 1659.

[2] The title of this ode was " The Political Ballance."

[3] The passage runs as follows :—

> " Lawgiving Ceres that inventing corn
> Is she, of whom bright Empire first was born,
> While men for Acorns tasting bread, began
> To parcel fields by laws Agrarian,
> And hence (as lots have chanc'd to rise or fall)
> Become the prize of One or Few or All."

This means, as will be seen when the theory is examined in chapter iii., that power depends on property, and that the number of the landowners determines whether the government is monarchial, oligarchic, or democratic.

in its composition. Hobbes appears to have started it, and it was continually hinted at by Stubbe, one of Harrington's chief literary opponents, who speaks of the " authors " and not the author of " Oceana." But it is of very little importance whether the rumour was true or not. As soon as the book was published and its doctrines popularised, the history of Harrington becomes merged in the history of the Harringtonians.

The publication of the work was not an easy matter. Thurloe's well-trained secret service got wind of its existence while it was passing through the press, and confiscated it. The year 1656 was not a happy year for authors who wished to promulgate doubtful doctrines. The Press Act of June 14, 1643 against which Milton had written " Areopagitica," the ordinance of September 28, 1647, Bradshaw's Act of September 20, 1649, renewed on January 7, 1653, and the further Order of the Council of September 5, 1655, were directed almost entirely against the anti-Cromwellian newspapers and prurient and indecent publications. Imprimaturs for books and pamphlets had not been hard to obtain, and both sides of most of the burning questions of the day had been stated with considerable freedom. But by the order of August 18, 1655, " against Scandalous Books and Pamphlets and for the Regulation of Printing," a much greater strictness was enforced, affecting the regular book trade.[1] Cromwell was gradually tightening the reins of his government ; he had instituted his system of major-generals ; and on November 27th he issued instructions for the suppression of the use of the Prayer Book in private houses. The greater stringency in dealing with the press was a part of this process

[1] Masson, " Life of Milton," v. 51, 60, 259, 351.

of extirpating opposition to his rule by measures of police.

The story told by Toland of how permission to print " Oceana " was finally obtained is a pretty one, illustrating Harrington's fondness for doing things in a picturesque way.   He won the father over by first getting at his favourite daughter. The Lady Claypole was the child of Cromwell's heart, and it was her early death that helped to hurry him to the grave.   She was generally able to get her way with her father.   As Toland wrote, " she acted the part of a Princess very naturally, obliging all persons with her civility, and frequently interceding for the unhappy."   " To this Lady, though an absolute stranger to him, he thought fit to make his application ; and being led into her Anti-chamber, he sent in his Name with his humble request that she would admit him to her presence.   While he attended, som of her Women coming into the room were followed by her little Daughter about three years old, who staid behind them.   He entertained the Child so divertingly, that she suffer'd him to take her up in his arms till her Mother came ; whereupon he stepping towards her, and setting the Child down at her feet, said ' Madam, 'tis well you are com at this nick of time, or I had certainly stolen this pretty little Lady.' " The mother was somewhat astonished and could not understand Harrington's behaviour, and she was no more enlightened when it was explained as a retaliation for Cromwell's theft of his own offspring.   But when she learnt that " Oceana " was meant, that the book had been misrepresented and contained nothing pre-judicial to Cromwell's government, she was won over, and having been promised one of the first copies, per-suaded her father to restore the confiscated material.

" Oceana " was finally published late in 1656, without the author's name.[1]   It was dedicated to the Protector, who was given the formidable task of converting England into Oceana and retiring into private life at the conclusion of his work, to die at the ripe age of one hundred and sixteen.

[1] It is advertised as newly published in " Mercurius Politicus," October 23 —November 6.   *Cf.* Firth, " Last Years of the Protectorate," i. 68.

CHAPTER II

" Oceana," the only one of his works by which Harrington is now remembered, is written in the form of a Utopia. This fact accounts for whatever notoriety it has to-day, as well as for the merriment with which it was received at the time of its composition. Utopias are generally regarded as literary curiosities which have been made respectable by illustrious names, rather than as serious contributions to the political problems which troubled the age at which they appeared. Plato, the greatest of all writers of Utopias, in some of the most pathetic words that were ever used in literature, acknowledged in the end that his suggestions were impracticable. " I don't think it exists anywhere on earth," he said of the Republic, " but perhaps in heaven it is set up as a pattern for him who will to gaze on and by his gaze to make himself like it. It doesn't matter, if it does or can exist." [1] More made no such apology, but as Chancellor of England he never attempted to introduce the reforms which he had sketched in " Utopia " into the country which he helped to govern. Harrington was at once classed in the same category as an unpractical idealist.

But " Oceana," although in the form of an ideal state, is a work of a different type from the " Republic " or " Utopia." It was meant neither for the skies nor for some spot on earth that did not exist, but for England. Its author had very clearly defined views

---

[1] Plato, " Republic," 592 B.

as to the needs of his country, and his love of the picturesque prompted him to bring them forward in the form of what he called a " political romance." The scene is laid in England, which appears as Oceana. The hero of the story is Cromwell, who under the pseudonym of Olphaus Megaletor is depicted as being troubled at night time by pondering over what a single man, Lycurgus, was able to do for Sparta. Fired by this example, he calls together a number of political scientists, and together they produce a new constitution. Cromwell is given a post not unlike that of Protector, and institutes the new order. He waits till the wheels are running smoothly, and finally retires into private life, leaving England the most prosperous and contented republic in the world. The book, stripped of its allegorical trappings, is little more than a magnified written constitution. Without having the poetical atmosphere of the legendary Utopia, it goes into details which a constitutional document does not presume to include, but it never leaves the political standpoint or wanders off into impossible suggestions that could not be realised in practice. It is a definite proposal for solving the difficulties in which England had become entangled since the abolition of monarchy, and one which its author hoped Cromwell might be induced to consider.

In presenting his theories in this guise and employing fictitious names, Harrington was adopting a literary trick not uncommon at the time. James Howell had, in 1645, written what he called an " allegorical discourse " which was " partly satirical," in which he had veiled various monarchs and countries of Europe under names coined from Latin or Greek words for trees, introducing into this setting discussions, not too serious, of the home and foreign politics of the day. " Dodona's Grove " met with extraordinary success and encouraged Howell to undertake a further attempt at this form of composition, " The Parley of Beasts," in which England appeared no longer as Druina, the land of the oak, but as Gheriona, the country of wool. Harrington must have been acquainted with Howell, the enthusiastic admirer of his cherished Venice, the first Englishman to write a work of any magnitude on its history and institutions,[1] and it is probable that he had him in mind when he presented the island state, the imperial ruler of the sea, the greater Venice, under the name of " Oceana." But it is clear that the concrete method of presenting political theory, which had already been employed in England by More and Bacon, was primarily due to the influence of the classics ; and it will be shown later that " Oceana " was probably inspired in particular by Plato's second best republic, " The Laws," which bears a similar resemblance to an elaborated written constitution.

The best of the so-called " Utopias " which were produced by the political ferment in England are undoubtedly those of Samuel Hartlib and Gerard Winstanley. " Macaria," written in 1641, is too short a work to be compared with " Oceana." It bears the mark of its author with his enthusiasm for agriculture and education on every page. Its main proposal consists of the formation of councils, five in number, to look after the material wants of the people, leaving all the other functions of government to education, for " the art of printing will so spread knowledge, that the common people, knowing their own rights and

---

[1] " A Survey of the Seignorie of Venice," 1651.   *Cf.* " Dodona's Grove," pp. 59-63, where Venice comes in for further praise under the name Adriana.

liberties, will not be governed by way of oppression ; and so, by little and little, all kingdoms will be like Macaria." [1] The production of Winstanley, the leader of the Diggers, entitled " The Law of Freedom in a Platform," [2] is a work on a larger scale, one of the most interesting and modern of the writings of the period. Many of its minor suggestions are very similar to those of Harrington, but Winstanley is an idealist without Harrington's restraining conservatism and grip of facts. His suggestions to abolish the Christian Church, and to do away with private property, place it far away from a work like " Oceana " among the ideal states to which the label Utopia has been less unreasonably attached.

The continuation of Bacon's " New Atlantis," and Sadler's " Olbia," both published after " Oceana," [3] bear little comparison with it. The one is an arrant plagiarism of More, the other the happy abode of dogmatic theology. " Oceana " stands alone as the only example of the type of literature that it represents, which has come down to us from the period of the Commonwealth outside the shelves of libraries ; and " Oceana " is almost miscalled a Utopia.

The author of this peculiar work, who has been aptly called the Sieyès of the English Rebellion,[4] was, like the famous French abbé, a conscious political theorist. The one thing which he postulated as the basis for the science of politics was the supremacy of laws and not of men. Men with their uncertainty and individuality upset the most careful of calculations : laws written in black and white and not subject to accident are the only things on which it is possible to

---

[1] " A Description of the Famous Kingdom of Macaria," 1641, Harl. Misc. i. 584.

[2] Written in 1651. [3] Both in 1660. [4] Burke, " Works," v. 242.

build.   Cromwell himself, though he resorted to a very stringent form of personal rule in his system of major-generals, was in agreement with Harrington up to a certain point.   He was one of the staunchest supporters of the idea of a fundamental law, which cannot be " unlawed." [1]   He accepted the Instrument of Government, and was the inspiration, if not the author, of the Humble Petition and Advice.   And all the opponents of the Stuart régime agreed that it had become essential to have some definite basis of government to prevent future disputes and uncertainties—some Greater Charter, which should be unalterable.   The realisation of this encouraged those who were interested in politics to enter the field in the hopes of winning a peculiar fame as framers of the constitution of England.

Those who opposed the idea of a written constitution took up a somewhat peculiar standpoint.   They rightly saw that, although Magna Carta gave it historical sanction, it was more directly due to the revived study of the classics.   In his " Behemoth " Hobbes laid much stress on the unhappy consequences of the Renaissance.[2]   He attributed half the trouble, through which England had passed, to the " gentlemen," who had brought their politics from the universities into the arena of public life, " having read the glorious histories and sententious politics of the ancient popular governments of the Greeks and Romans, amongst whom Kings were branded with the names of tyrants and popular governments . . . passed by the name of liberty." [3] " The core of rebellion," he added later, with almost prophetic insight into subsequent European history,

[1] *Cf*. Speech III. in Carlyle, " Cromwell's Letters and Speeches."
[2] " Behemoth," Masseres Tracts, pp. 478, 497, 605, 608.
[3] *Ibid*. p. 478.

" (as you have seen by this and read of other rebellions),
is in the universities." [1]   The democratising influence
of the classics was in the seventeenth century a
commonplace argument ;   nearly all the democratic
ideas of the time may be, in fact, paralleled from
Greek and Roman writers ; but the most striking of all
of them was this idea of the fundamental law or written
constitution, which was so inseparably connected with
the republican movement.

But objection was not confined to the actual
teachings of Greece and Rome : the method used by
the classical historians and political writers was also
criticised.   Harrington was ridiculed by Hobbes for
following them, because living under popular states
" they derived those rights not from the Principles
of Nature, but transcribed them into their books
out of the practice of their own Commonwealths, as
Grammarians describe the Rules of Language out
of Poets." [2]

Strong arguments, as will be shown later, were
brought forward against Harrington's doctrines, but
his method was the wrong thing to find fault with.
Here he stood on firm ground.   He knew that his
strength lay in his grip of fact and his knowledge of
the " practice of Commonwealths "—his use of the
inductive method.   His opponents could urge that
" it is the Foundation of Government upon undeniable
Principles and the Deductions from them, which render
Politiques a complete Science, without which the
greatest Conversation with particular Commonwealths
can but at most make men Empiricals at policy." [3]
But he was ready with his answer, a comparison
between himself and " famous Hervy."   The circulation

---

[1] " Behemoth," p. 511.   [2] " Oceana," p. 38.
[3] Wren, " Monarchy asserted," etc., 1660, E. 1853.

of the blood was a medical fact before it was discovered by Harvey ; but an experimental study of
anatomy and a departure from the deductive methods
of medical science were necessary in order that this
generalisation could be reached.   The inductive
method necessitates the formation of some principle,
to guide the seeker in his choice of facts, no less than
the deductive method.   Harrington had his principles
no less than Hobbes or Filmer, but he arrived at them
by a historical method.   By reading English history
with intelligence and comparing it with ancient and
modern European history he came to the conclusion
that there were two main things wrong with England,
the balance of property and the working of the parliamentary system.   By arranging his facts he was then
able to formulate his two great political principles,
that the preservation of states has in the past depended, and probably still depends, on the preservation
of the Balance of Property and on Rotation in Government.   Harrington did not claim to have introduced
a new factor into politics any more than Harvey did
into medicine.   He claimed to be a political scientist
and not a political poet.   It was entirely in consonance
with his historical method that he omitted to allude
to the doctrine of the social contract, which monarchists
as well as republicans brought forward with much
confidence and regularity.
    The historical method was comparatively new to
English political thought.   Harrington carried it to
its extreme, considering it imperfect, unless supplemented by a practical knowledge of contemporary
foreign politics.   " No man," he wrote in " Oceana,"
" can be a Politician, except he be first a Historian or
a Traveller." [1]   But in his enthusiasm for history and

---

[1] " Oceana," p. 183.

travel he did not omit to study his predecessors in the line of research, to which he devoted his life's work. He had an extraordinary instinct for selecting for imitation the particular political writers, whom posterity has accepted as genuine contributors to political science. The three names which occur most frequently in his writings are the three which are generally regarded as the greatest lights of the century and a half preceding him—those of Bacon, Grotius, and Machiavelli. Machiavelli is to Harrington " the greatest artist in the modern world," " the Prince of Politicians," " the only Politician of later ages," " the sole retriever of this ancient prudence." " He that will erect a Commonwealth against the Judgment of Machiavel is obliged to give such reasons for his enterprise as must not go a-begging." [1] This worship of Machiavelli is in itself no extraordinary thing. Sir Walter Raleigh had a somewhat similar admiration for him. But if it is remembered that Machiavelli was hardly ever alluded to in the seventeenth century except as a synonym for all that is vicious and immoral in public life,[2] and, when he was defended, it was as an unfortunate Italian who lived in bad times,[3] the fact carries a new significance. Harrington, although the writer of an ideal Commonwealth, saw that doctrinaire or no doctrinaire, a politician must stand upon the ground of fact. Before him Machiavelli had been almost alone in recognising this. Scholars had so far departed from this method that, until the awakening

---

[1] " Oceana," pp. 38, 52, 147, 149, etc.

[2] According to Edward Meyer ("Machiavelli and the Elizabethan Drama ") the popular view of Machiavelli is to be explained by the fact that his principles were known to English readers mainly through a misrepresentation of him written by a Frenchman, Gentillet, in 1576, and translated into English in the following year. None of his own works except " The Art of War " and " The History of Florence " were translated till 1636.

[3] *Cf.* Francis Osborn, " Works," ii. 77.

which both produced and was produced by Machiavelli, they based their theories not on facts, but on
the thinker who above all others exemplified their
importance—Aristotle. Harrington, like Machiavelli,
revived the true Aristotle and assisted in crushing
Aristotelianism.

Not the least important service rendered by Harrington was the application of this historical method
to Scripture. The illogical use of biblical parallels,
which was made by monarchists and Puritans alike,
was of a striking nature. Arguing that practices which
were valuable in scriptural times must be valuable
for their own day, they were unwilling to accept anything which had not the sacred commendation of
chapter and verse. " Bishops are now unfit to govern
because of their learning," said Selden in words which
barely caricature the facts; " they are bred up in
another law, they run to the text for something done
amongst the Jews that nothing concerns England, 'tis
just as if a man would have a kettle and he would not
go to our brazier to have it made as they make kettles,
but he would have it made, as Hiram made his brass
work, who wrought in Solomon's temple." [1] Harrington quietly neglected this method and, as Grotius
and Machiavelli had done before him, attempted to
treat the political system of the Jews on the same
lines as the constitutions of Athens, Sparta, or Rome.
As a politician the Bible was to him nothing more
than the history of the Jewish Commonwealth. He
was undoubtedly interested in his researches in biblical
politics, seeing in the tribal organisation of the
Israelites a very striking example of a far-reaching
and successful agrarian law. But he also wished to
turn the weapons of the monarchist divines against

[1] Selden, " Table Talk," English Reprints, 1868, p. 26.

themselves. The Divine Right of Kings, the monarchy of Saul and Melchisedec, Christ's command to "render unto Cæsar the things which be Cæsar's, and to God the things that are God's," were exploited by all the supporters of absolute monarchy. Harrington replied with a historical account of the republican institutions of the Jews, which, though dull and sometimes pedantic, served as an answer to the monarchists and an argument for republicanism to their Puritan opponents.

But Jewish history, although for these peculiar reasons important, was with Harrington subordinate to both classical and modern history. Both these branches of study were under the influence of men like himself being applied to politics. Works like the "Oration of Agrippa to Octavius Cæsar Augustus against Monarchy," were translated.[1] Writings on Spanish, Portuguese, Dutch, French, Ottoman, German, and Italian history poured forth from the press in the form of pamphlets. The list of places to which reference was made ranged from Pegu to Ragusa.[2] Special attention was paid to Venice. Howell's book was followed in 1658 by the Earl of Monmouth's translation of Paruta's "History." Nothing was neglected by Harrington ; but it was above all to the cities of the ancient world that he looked. "Oceana" was discovered not in "phansy" but in "the archives of antient prudence."[3]

A writer who relies on the comparative and historical method, even if he is framing a Utopia, will in all probability not produce a work of art. Harrington was no stylist. Hume classed him with Bacon and Milton as "altogether stiff and pedantic."[4]

---

[1] E. 779 in the British Museum Catalogue.
[2] *Cf.* the pamphlet on the government of Ragusa in E. 985.
[3] "Oceana," p. 79.   [4] Hume, Essay XII.

Although it is not necessary to accept either this classification or this verdict, yet it must be acknowledged that Harrington can bear no comparison with many writers of his age for splendour and ease of diction. For epigrams and flashes of picturesque expression he was unrivalled ; and his use of biblical language could be very effective,[1] but the purple patches are separated by passages of a very wearisome nature. It is by his political thought and not by his art that he must be judged. We may not endorse Toland's opinion that he is " an Author who far outdoes all that went before him, in his exquisit knowledge of the Politics."[2] We may reject Hume's further judgment accepted with reservation by Maitland,[3] that " the Oceana is the only valuable model of a commonwealth that has yet been offered to the public."[4] We may refuse to follow Coleridge in classing him along with Thucydides, Tacitus, Machiavelli, and Bacon, as one of the " red letter names even in the almanacs of worldly wisdom."[5] But the least enthusiastic cannot help paying some tribute to his clear thought and undoubted political instinct.

[1] " Oceana is as the Rose of Sharon, and the Lilly of the Vally. As the Lilly among Thorns, such is my Love among the Daughters. She is comly as the Tents of Kedar, and terrible as an Army with Banners. Her neck is as the tower of David, builded for an Armory, whereon there hang a thousand Bucklers and Shields of mighty Men. Let me hear thy Voice in the morning whom my soul loves." ("Oceana," p. 203.)

[2] Preface to Harrington's " Works," xxvii.

[3] Maitland, " Collected Papers," i. 22.   [4] Hume, Essay XVI.

[5] Coleridge, " Statesman's Manual," p. 20. Wordsworth's lines may be compared :

> " Great men have been among us ; hands that penned
> And tongues that uttered wisdom—better none !
> The later Sidney, Marvell, Harrington,
> Young Vane, and others who called Milton friend."

CHAPTER III

THE POLITICAL IDEAS OF *OCEANA*

§ I

HARRINGTON'S political theory is comprised in two fundamental propositions, on which all the other suggestions which are embodied in his writings are built. (i) The preservation of a state depends on the possession of an adequate proportion of the land by the ruling class. (ii) Government cannot remain pure and healthy without the assistance of four mechanical contrivances—the ballot, indirect election, rotation, and a system of two chambers in which the functions of debating and voting are kept separate. For the first of these proposals Harrington claimed originality ; he did not conceal the fact that the second was borrowed from various sources.

The theory of the " balance of property " explained in the dictum, " As is the proportion or balance of Dominion or Property in Land, such is the nature of the Empire," [1] and claimed by Harrington as his own peculiar discovery, has met with general acceptation. Bonar ascribes the importance of " Oceana " to its " new principle that the economical element in a state will determine its government." [2] Cornwall Lewis includes among the general true propositions of politics " that the seat of power in any state is dependent on the preponderance of property." [3] Thorold Rogers counts it " a common-place in practical politics

---

[1] " Oceana," p. 39.   [2] " Philosophy of Political Economy," p. 90.
[3] " A Treatise on Politics," ii. 46.

that they who own the land of a country make its laws." [1]   The political importance of the possession of the land had been recognised from the time when Joseph made his investments in property before the Egyptian famine.   The institution of the Jubilee among the Jews, the reforms of Lycurgus and Solon, the work of the Gracchi, of Julius Cæsar, and the later Roman Emperors, as well as the whole feudal system depended on the practical recognition of this fact.   But no political writer before Harrington had been conscious of a principle illustrated by so many isolated facts.   No one had developed a theory.

In 1647, at the important debates which took place over the propositions of the Agreement of the People, the thesis that power *ought* to depend on property was urged by Ireton and the more conservative of the officers with the greatest persistence.[2]   The position maintained by the democrats and voiced by their spokesman, Colonel Rainsborough, was " that the poorest He that is in England hath a life to live as well as the greatest He ; and therefore . . . every man that is to live under a government ought, first, by his own consent, to put himself under that government." Ireton in reply used the argument that is always used on the other side in this eternal problem.   Only those deserve a vote who " have a permanent fixed interest in the kingdom . . . the persons in whom all land lies and those in corporations in whom all trading lies."   For, if by the law of nature every man has a " right " to elect his governor, he has by the same dangerous law the " right of self-pre-servation," which means the right to procure food

---

[1] " The Economic Interpretation of History," p. 163.

[2] Clarke Papers, i. 299-345.

and clothes and to have a piece of land, on which to live.[1] If this is granted, what becomes of private property ? The preservation of property was the chief article of Ireton's political creed, and the obvious means of securing it was to confine the government of the country to owners of private property—those who have a fixed interest in the country.[2]

While Ireton was trying to show why this class of people ought to govern, Harrington was beginning to discover that they *do* govern. It was a fact which he could not explain away, and a fact which was of some importance to the discussions which have been described. When he came to publish his discovery and illustrate it in concrete form in his ideal state, Harrington never explained the exact way in which the landed classes exercise their power. He did not, like Vane, propose to ensure the connection between property and government by confining the franchise to owners of property in land.[3] He proposed, it is true, the abolition of the borough constituencies ; but he permitted owners of property of all kinds to exercise their vote. His affirmation that force has not got the last word in politics, and his blunt picture of an army (" that is a beast that has a big belly and must be fed ") depending ultimately for its support upon the land, seems to show that he was thinking of something

[1] The outcome of this particular argument was the fundamental against levelling in the final draft of the Agreement.

[2] In one passage Ireton almost expressed Harrington's principle that property *does* govern. " If this man will live in this Kingdom or trade amongst us, that man ought to subject himself to the law made by the people, who have the interest of this Kingdom in us ; and yet I do acknowledge that which you take to be so general a maxim, that in every kingdom, the original of power, of making laws, of determining what shall be law in the land, does lie in the people that are possessed of the permanent interest of the land." (Clarke Papers, i. 319.)

[3] " Commons Journals," vii. 223.

more concrete than the franchise, an economic rather than a political force.[1]

There can be little doubt that Harrington was first led in the direction of his famous principle by his study of the Roman historians, in whose pages agrarian laws play so large a part. But events had been happening nearer home, which might well have turned his mind in this direction.

The hostility of the Irish people had been a cause of constant alarm to English statesmen, and since the middle of the sixteenth century an attempt more or less continuous and systematic had been made to Anglicise Ireland by settling men of English birth upon the land. This policy was given a more definite form by the Confiscation Act of 1642, which foreshadowed the later Cromwellian settlement. By this settlement, the details of which were arranged in numerous Acts, about eleven-twentieths of the total land of Ireland, which had previously been in the hands of the Crown, the Church, or rebels, was declared to be forfeited and divided among the adventurers, the army, and the creditors of the Commonwealth. All Irishmen who could not prove a " constant good affection " to the Parliament were transplanted into Connaught. It was estimated that between 1656 and 1659, 32,000 Englishmen were placed on Irish soil, while in the longer period between 1641 and 1687, 2,400,000 acres of land were transferred from Roman Catholics to Protestants.[2] The settlement was carried out under the direction of Sir William Petty, who was afterwards a friend of Harrington ; and Harrington himself

---

[1] " Oceana," p. 41.
[2] Fitzmaurice, " Life of Sir William Petty," pp. 51 and 65 ; Hull, " The Economic Writings of Sir William Petty," ii. 606.

was financially interested in it, having a considerable sum of money invested in Irish land.[1] He would thus have further reasons for watching a scheme which was based so clearly on the principle which he himself was tabulating. In "Oceana" (after a flippant suggestion to plant Ireland with the Jews of Europe) he took the opportunity of expressing his approval of Cromwell's policy on the ground that it made for peace.[2]

The other movement, which must have influenced Harrington in the formation of his principle, has already been alluded to. The sect of Diggers had created no small stir in the year 1649 by attempting to cultivate the commons in various parts of South England. A contemporary pamphlet gives the following description of them.[3] "As his Excellency the Lord General came from Gilford to London, he went to view the Diggers at St Geo. Hill in Surrey, with his officers and attendants, where they found about 12 of them hard at work and amongst them one Winstanley was the chief speaker to whom several questions were propounded by the officers, and the Lord General made a short speech by way of admonition to them and this Winstanley returned sober answers, though they gave little satisfaction (if any at all) in regard of the strangeness of the action. It was urged that the commons were as justly due to the Lords as any other lands. They answered that these were Crown Lands, where they digged, and that the king that possessed them by the Norman Conquest being dead, they were returned again to the common people of

[1] Prendergast, "Cromwellian Settlement," 2nd ed., p. 431.

[2] "Oceana," p. 111. I can find no evidence for the suggestion made in Lord Fitzmaurice's "Life of Sir William Petty" (p. 23), that Cromwell's Irish policy was inspired by Harrington's theory.

[3] "The Speeches of the Lord General Fairfax . . . to the Diggers," 1649, E. 530.

England, who might improve them, if they would take the pains, that for those who would come dig with them, they should have the benefit equal with them and eat of their bread, but they would not force any, applying all to the golden rule, to do to others as we would be done unto ; some officers wished they had no further plot in what they did, and that no more was intended than what they did pretend."

The movement, as indeed may be seen from this passage, was not purely political. Like the modern Socialism, it was also ethical. Rightly or wrongly, the Diggers were accused of free love ; and not only in common with all the popular party did they deliver bitter attacks on the clergy, but they were in favour of substituting a natural and secular religion for Christianity.[1] But the political aspect of their communism is what affects the present argument. They defined liberty as the freedom of the earth.[2] They believed that the Norman kings recognised this view when " they took possession of the earth for their *freedom,*" and they went on to argue that the victory of the Commoners was useless, unless they asserted the liberty which they had won with their swords and in their turn " took possession of the earth." Acting upon these principles they attacked two institutions in particular—the rights of the lords of the manor and the laws of primogeniture, which excluded all younger sons from any share in the family property,[3] and in the case of the former their protest assumed the practical form of digging up the common lands. The movement was perhaps small and unimportant, but it

[1] *Cf.* Winstanley, " The Law of Freedom in a Platform," chap. iv.
[2] *Ibid.* chap. i.
[3] *Ibid.* pp. 60-62

was one which was calculated to attract the attention of a lover of the curious like the author of " Oceana."

In this atmosphere, then, Harrington arrived at his first proposition, " as is the proportion or balance of Dominion or Property in Land, such is the nature of the Empire." When a single person is sole proprietor of a country's land, the government will be monarchical ; when a limited number share it with him, the government will be that of a mixed monarchy ; when the people own the soil, the government will be democratic. In this simple proposition Harrington saw the cause of the enormous upheaval in England and its remedy.

He traced the Civil War back to the policy of the Tudors. Henry VII. began the mischief with the Statutes of Population, Retainers and Alienation, which broke up the great estates of the barons and brought about a condition of affairs under which " the great Tables of the Nobility . . . no longer nourished veins that would bleed for them."[1] Henry VIII. continued his father's work by dissolving the monasteries and giving their lands to men of new families. Elizabeth, " converting her reign thro the perpetual love-tricks that past between her and her People into a kind of Romance,"[2] postponed the inevitable outcome of these measures. But under the Stuarts it became apparent that the monarchy had not got the necessary support to maintain its power, and it gave place to the Commonwealth. The continuation of this policy by Cromwell in the wholesale confiscation of the land of Crown, Church, and Royalist partisans pointed more and more to the necessity of democratic institutions for England.

[1] " Oceana," p. 69.   [2] Ibid. p. 69.

In pre-Tudor days, when the land was in the possession of a few barons and dignitaries of the Church dependent on the Crown, the natural form of government was a regulated monarchy; but with the enormous increase in the number of landowners, monarchical institutions had finally become impossible.

There were two ways of remedying this fact and bringing about the coincidence of power and property. The government might be changed to suit the changed balance of property, or the balance of property could be changed so as to make the old form of government again possible. Harrington himself was of opinion that it was easier to change the form of government than to revert to old economic conditions, and was for this among other reasons the most uncompromising republican of his age.

Accepting as he did the altered economic conditions, he set out to formulate proposals which should establish the new government in greater security and render it more like the cities of Greek and Roman history that he so much admired. His proposals were intended to be enforced in an agrarian law, which he tabulated for his idealised England—Oceana. By this measure the policy of breaking up large estates was to be pushed one stage further. The details were to be arranged after a valuation of the land had been made,[1] but the provisional idea was to allow no one to possess land above the value of £2000 in England and Ireland, or £500 in Scotland, where the risk of the soil being monopolised by a few chieftains was especially great. Harrington estimated the total rent of the land of England and Wales at ten million

[1] " Oceana," p. 110.

pounds,[1] so that the total number of landowners would never fall below five thousand. It would probably be far larger in view of the absurdity of imagining five thousand men clinging to the possession of the exact maximum legally allowed to them, with everybody else looking on. But Harrington was not desirous of introducing a too sudden or drastic change. He therefore recommended that this breaking up of estates should be brought about quite gradually.

There was one obvious method of achieving this. Interest in the question of the inheritance of estates had not been confined to the Diggers. A book entitled the " Apology for the Younger Brother," or " The Younger Brother's Plea," had appeared from an Oxford press in 1636, and from 1641 to 1647 William Somner had been writing his " Treatise of Gavelkind." [2] Both these men attacked the system of land-tenure which had been in vogue in England since the Norman Conquest, and proposed that the father should be allowed to divide his property among all his children or dispose of it as he might think best. The many favourable comments in the fugitive literature of the period show that there was a certain amount of feeling on the question ; the resolution of the Long Parliament (1645), converting military tenures into soccage, which was already devisable, points in the same direction ; and great stimulus was given to the whole movement by the account which travellers gave of its successful working in the Netherlands.

Harrington therefore (himself an eldest son) proposed the abolition of this relic of feudalism as the

---

[1] "The Art of Lawgiving," p. 457.   Petty's estimate was eight millions See Hull, " The Economic Writings of Sir W. Petty," i. 105.

[2] It was not published till 1659.

least violent way of dividing the large estates. He
supplemented it with two other proposals. He would
forbid men who owned property worth £2000 or more
to make a further acquisition by purchase, and he
would restrict marriage portions to £1500. But with
his belief in moderation he would not forbid acquisi-
tions by legacy, and he made it clear that his agrarian
law would only come into force in the case of children born seven years or more after its passing. His
explanation that such a course would not " bring
any man from the customs to which he has been
inur'd, nor from any emergent expectations he may
have," [1] reads like a passage from the individualist-
utilitarians of the nineteenth century. This proposal,
far less radical than many proposals of the time, had
the merits of brevity and clearness. It was defended
on the grounds that a further partition of the land
was necessary to secure the new republic in its democratic institutions.

The ideal which Harrington had before him in
making this suggestion was, as he tells us,[2] the agri-
cultural democracy which Aristotle had commended,
or Rome in the simple brilliant days, when her generals
left their ploughs for the battlefield. He was himself
a country gentleman with a passion for the land,
who took pride in the particular genius of the English
people with their " aversion to the ways of the Court "
and their " country way of life," [3] and he hoped that
certain social changes would follow his political
reforms. The clergy and the lawyers were classes
odious to the more radical sections of the popular

---

[1] " The Art of Lawgiving," p. 457. In his later pamphlets Harrington
made such trifling additions to his theories that I have not hesitated to quote
from these, as though they were written in the same year as " Oceana."

[2] "Oceana," p. 178.

[3] *Ibid.* p. 35.

party.[1]   Both were supporters of the monarchy. Both depended for their existence on expert knowledge and acquaintance with what was thought to be unnecessary and deceptive lore.   Both were foes to land, the clergy as monopolising a great part of it, the lawyers as responsible for all the obstructions put in the way of purchasers.   Their numbers had been very largely recruited from the younger sons of gentle families, who had no opportunity of leading the life of country gentlemen.   By giving every son the right to inherit a part of his father's estate, Harrington hoped that the obnoxious classes of clergy and lawyers would be curtailed and converted into an additional class of country gentlemen which would be to Oceana almost what the guardians were to Plato's Republic.

In his " Discourses "[2] Machiavelli had written the following passage.   " I call those Gentlemen who live idly and plentifully upon their estates without any care or employment, and they are very pernicious, wherever they are . . . it would be impossible to erect a republic where they had the Dominion."   In one respect the pupil did not follow his master.   Like Sir Thomas Smith (whose book he had read), who was of opinion that " gentlemen are made good cheap in

[1] The following stanza in the song of the Diggers (1649) is noteworthy :—
" Gainst Lawyers and gainst Priests stand up now, stand up now.
Gainst Lawyers and gainst Priests, stand up now,
For tyrants they are both even flat against their oath.
To grant us they are loath free meat and drink and cloth.
Stand up now, Diggers all." [1]
It may be compared with Harrington's verdict of the two classes as " irreconcilable enemies of popular power," [2] and his observation " With absolute Monarchy and with Aristocracy it is an innat Maxim that the People are to be deceived in two things, their Religion and their Law." [3]
[2] Machiavelli, "Works," 1657 edition, p. 325.

[1] Clarke Papers, ii. 223.   [2] " The Art of Lawgiving," p. 432.
[3] " A System of Politics," p. 509.

England," [1] and like Cromwell himself who was proud
of being a gentleman [2] and had said " A nobleman,
a gentleman, a yeoman, that is a good interest of the
Nation and a great one." Harrington believed in
the upper classes. The word " gentleman " meant
to him all that " ἀγαθὸς " meant to the Greek, all that
" buoni uomini " meant to the Italian, all that
" meliores " meant to the English merchant.[3] He
pointed out that all the great legislators from Moses
down to Cromwell had been " gentlemen " and gave it
as his firm opinion that : " There is something first
in the making of a Commonwealth, then in the governing of it, and last of all in the leading of its Armys ;
which (tho' there be great Divines, great lawyers,
great men in all professions) seems to be peculiar only
to the genius of a Gentleman." [4] He believed that
there was no such thing as a pure democracy [5]—
especially in a nation possessing a natural aristocracy
of country gentlemen—and his instincts brought
arguments to support his opinion.

These sympathies, however admirable, gave
Harrington a somewhat narrow and limited outlook.
The age in which he lived is important among other
reasons for the remarkable expansion of English trade,
which was beginning to take place. It marks the
commencement of the commercial era in the nation's
history. Harrington was not altogether blind to the
requirements of the commercial and industrial form of

[1] " De Republica Anglorum," chap. xx. Smith however counts lawyers
as gentlemen.
[2] Carlyle, Speech III.
[3] Even in New England there was the same respect for the class. Osgood
remarks that " the order of magistracy and the rank of gentleman were
considered very nearly synonymous," " American Colonies in the Seventeenth
Century," i. 178. And in the Body of Liberties of the colony special provisions
were made to prevent the infliction of corporal punishment on " gentlemen "
[4] " Oceana," p. 56. [5] *Ibid.* p. 48.

community. He did not rise above the mercantile theory; but by his brief remarks on the investment of capital[1] and by his introduction of a Council of Trade amongst the institutions of "Oceana" he showed that he was alive to the importance of the commercial development. Furthermore the democratising influence of trade did not escape his notice. "Where there is a bank," he argues, "ten to one there is a Commonwealth. A King is a Soldier or a Lover, neither of which makes a good merchant and without Merchandise you will have a lean Bank."[2] Nevertheless he did not extend his principle beyond landed property except in certain cases. In one passage he explained that "in such cities as subsist mostly by Trade, and have little or no land, as Holland and Genoa, the balance of Treasure may be equal to that of Land in the cases mentioned,"[3] and in another passage he excepted from his general proposition primitive societies, into which private property has not been introduced, states of small territory but enormous commerce, and little countries, where estates are not large enough to exceed other forms of wealth.[4] But he adhered to his main assertion that power follows the balance of landed property, and saw no reason to extend it in the case of England. His work would have been of greater value if he had applied it to the industrial form of community, but, before Harrington is condemned, three points should be taken into consideration. (i) He had lived much of his life in dreams of the old days of Greece and Rome, and was not unnaturally influenced by the position which the commercial classes had occupied in the ancient city state. (ii) He did not desire to illustrate the larger truth, which was already sufficiently

[1] "The Prerogative of Popular Government," p. 246.   [2] *Ibid.* p. 247.
[3] "Oceana," p. 40.   [4] "The Prerogative of Popular Government," p. 247.

recognised, that riches mean power.   (iii) Up to the middle of the seventeenth century the trade of England had been confined largely to wool, the connection of which with the land need hardly be pointed out.

A doctrinaire is apt to overstate his case.   The possession of land may not have such important political results as Harrington thought.   Because property in land is " the most hooded and ty'd to the Perch," it does not follow that it is the most influential form of wealth ; and it is open to dispute that a nation's territories correspond to an individual's purse. Harrington may have laid stress upon the economic causes of the Civil War at the expense of the political, religious, and intellectual causes.   But his general position was sound.   The value of the economic view of history has, until recent times, been under-estimated. Harrington was one of the first writers to give to economic considerations the prominence that they deserve and to bring them into connection with the science of politics.   The long duration of the sovereignty of the Whig landowners no less than the modern socialist propaganda for the nationalisation of the land bears eloquent testimony to the soundness of his actual thesis.

§ 2

Harrington's policy with regard to the land was meant to achieve two objects.   By his socialistic division of property he hoped to make republican institutions possible.   By keeping power in the hands of the steadier section of the community, which is engaged in agriculture, he hoped to avoid the extreme form of democracy.

The four suggestions which must now be dealt with, the ballot, indirect election, rotation, and the separation of the functions of debating and voting have

the same twofold aspect. At the same time, as safe-
guarding the nation against an oligarchic form of
tyranny, they are meant to keep it from passing to
unrestrained licence and anarchy. In a word they
are contrivances for creating a democracy, but a democracy with checks. Similar ideas were to be found
in many of the cities of Italy, Germany, Switzerland,
and the Netherlands, in ecclesiastical institutions,
in academic societies, and in gilds and companies.
Harrington, with an audacity that gives him a claim to
originality, proposed to extend them to national politics
and embody them in his new constitution of England.

The ballot, a term used to represent election by
lot almost as frequently as election by secret vote,[1]
was directed against two separate evils, disorder and
bribery. It is important to realise this in assigning
Harrington his proper position in the history of political
theory. The use of written votes, the practice of
making a " scratch " or a " prick " on a written list,
the custom of placing papers, beans, balls, bullets,
pellets, tickets or coins into a box, trunk, urn, glass,
chalice, or even hat, which we find in elections held
at the chapter-house, abbey, college, and city hall, was
in many cases accompanied with no sort of secrecy.[2]
The regulations make it quite clear that in many
cases nothing more was attempted than to secure a
quiet and methodical election ; and sometimes to
ensure against the possibilities of fraud which accompany secrecy, the voting was publicly announced at
the conclusion of the election.[3] At Venice on the other

---

[1] Cf. "The Art of Lawgiving," pp. 403, 425, etc.

[2] The practice (common at Oxford and Cambridge) of whispering one's vote
in the ear of the " scrutator " is a good instance of a method of election which
aimed at no more than partial secrecy.

[3] This was perhaps most noticeable at Cambridge. Cf. Heywood,
" Cambridge Statues of the Sixteenth Century," p. 101 and passim.

hand, and at papal elections, where the close imprisonment of the cardinals was followed by the burning of
their votes, it is equally clear that the sole object of all
the electoral ritual was the prevention of corruption,
which is always possible where voting is public.[1]

We know that in proposing the introduction of
the ballot Harrington was chiefly inspired by the
example of Venice, which was the only modern state
for which he had a genuine admiration. The Venetian
constitution, which boasted a longer life than any
other in Christendom, aroused considerable interest
in England at this time.   In 1644 a number of members
of Parliament had applied to the Venetian ambassador
for an account of its institutions.   Raleigh and Howell,
whose writings were widely read, were enthusiastic
in its praise, and allusions to it in some form or other
occur with very great frequency in contemporary
pamphlets.   But people were not ready to shower
unthinking praise upon it. Sir Henry Wotton, who
had been ambassador at Venice from 1604 to 1610
and from 1616 to 1619, had indulged in biting criticism
in his letters to various eminent men.[2] The "most
serene republique" was commonly blamed for its
tyrannical and oligarchic features,[3] and its success
was attributed to its geographical position and the
perpetual engagement in warlike enterprises, which
guarded it from internal distractions.[4]

The ballot was not a remedy which would meet

---

[1] The same provision for burning the votes was in force at Pembroke
College, Oxford.

[2] Pearsall Smith, " Sir Henry Wotton, Life and Letters," i. 55, 113 ; ii.
121, 136-7, 228 and *passim.*

[3] *Cf.* Filmer, " Observations on Aristotle's Politiques touching forms of
government."

[4] *Cf.* Nedham, " Excellency of a Free State," pp. 62-3.   Wren's " Considerations on Mr Harrington's Oceana, " Preface, and " Monarchy asserted,"
p. 70.   Burton " Diary," iii. 151, etc.

with general approval. It had been tried in Massachusetts and Connecticut.[1] In our own House of
Commons the Presbyterians in 1646 had proposed
the appointment of a committee to " consider of a
Balloting Box and the use of it " in view of the election of certain officials. And in the election held on
February 1st, 1650, to fill the vacancies in the Council
of State, the twenty new members had been chosen
by some form of ballot. But it was in reality a new
departure for national politics. It was a device that
was connected in men's minds with close corporations.
It was all very well for Gresham College, the Royal
College of Physicians, the Virginia Company, the
Clothworkers and other livery companies in London
or Paris.[2] It was excusable for vestry meetings,[3]
papal, canonical, and academic elections.[4] It was
suitable enough for Venice, Emden, Angers and all
the other little aristocracies of the continent. It
was even possible for a little English town like Wisbech.[5]
But no one ventured to suggest the extension of this
municipal device to a great nation like England.

The indirect method of election, which has so often
been suggested at the same time as the ballot, was
common in various forms in the Dutch and Italian

[1] For its history in Connecticut see an article by S. E. Baldwin in the
American Historical Association, " Papers," vol. iv.

[2] For London the Bye-Laws of the various Companies may be consulted;
for Paris the section on " Les Métiers et Corporations " in the " Histoire
générale de Paris," René de Lespinasse.

[3] Cf. Webb, " English Local Government," Parish and County, p. 108n.,
Manor and Borough, p. 271.

[4] Cf. " On the three ways of canonical election." J. W. Legg.

[5] Cf. W. Watson, " Historical account of the town of Wisbech," pp. 230-33,
and " Reports from Commissioners on Municipal Corporations in England
and Wales," iv. 2552.

At Swansea, Boston, Deal, Faversham, Fordwich, Lincoln, Romsey,
Southampton, and some other places, forms of secret voting were introduced
at a more or less early stage in their municipal histories. Cf. ibid. i. 386; ii.
743, 874, 931, 965, 987; iv. 2346, 2152 and 2157.

cities and in the various commercial and ecclesiastical corporate bodies. Sometimes committees were appointed, elected, or chosen by lot to act as an electoral body ; sometimes the body that nominated candidates for offices was different from the body that made the election ; in Venice at the election of the Doge no fewer than ten stages of the most elaborate nature had to be passed in order to reach the requisite degree of indirectness. It was not unknown in England. In all the various forms of election which had been tried in choosing the Lord Mayor and the aldermen in the city of London it was employed.[1] In 1647 the army had chosen their " agitators " indirectly. By the scheme of the Fifth Monarchy in 1649 Church Parliaments were to be elected by means of delegates. And in Scotland the grouped boroughs elected their members by sending representatives chosen from each separate borough. Nevertheless, like the ballot, the indirect form of election was a device that was connected primarily with the university, the chapter-house, and the company, and the elaborate little city states on the continent.

The devices of the ballot and indirect election had been directed chiefly against the disorder and corruption, with which electors are beset. The other two devices, rotation and Harrington's peculiar form of double-chamber government, were directed against the similar temptations of elected persons.

The central idea of rotation or alternation in office is clear enough. The belief that " the prolongation of magistracy is the ruin of popular government " lay at the root of Greek and Roman institutions.[2] The same theory suggested the brief tenure of office

[1] *Cf.* H. K. S. Causton, " Elections in the City of London," ccxl. etc.
[2] " Pian Piano," p. 561.

common in the Italian republics of the Middle Ages,
where (with the single exception of Venice) magistracies
were never held for more than a year, and seldom for
more than two or three months.   Parallel to this,
though less radical, was the Self-Denying Ordinance
of 1645, and the proposals for annual, biennial, and
triennial parliaments made respectively by the Diggers
in their various manifestoes, the authors of the schemes
known as " The Heads of the Proposals," and " The
Agreement of the People," and the supporters of
" The Instrument of Government."   Short tenure of
office has always been considered so essential to the
democratic ideal that no more need here be said
about it.

It is obvious, however, that a certain instability
must accompany frequent changes of government.
And the question which democrats had to answer
was how can this instability be avoided ?   There
were two methods which had been tried in various
Dutch and French towns and in nearly all the merchant
companies of which we know.[1]   It could be arranged
either that one or more of the officers who would
naturally be dismissed should be retained in office
for an additional term, in order to instruct their
successors and maintain a certain amount of continuity
in policy, or else that the government should be
renovated by detachments so that there would always
be some men of experience and some novices in office.
The former method had been suggested in two connections in England.   Before the dissolution of the
Long Parliament it had been proposed to permit the
existing members to retain their seats, but to elect a
new body to share the government with them.   And

---

[1] For the French towns see Babeau, " La Ville sous l'ancien régime,"
pp. 50-69.   For the Dutch towns cf. Davies, " Holland," i. 79, etc.

when the Council of State was renewed certain old
members retained office in company with the fresh
men supplied by Parliament. The other method,
which was common enough in the gilds and merchant
companies, had never been tried in our national
politics. It had, however, been proposed either in
1650 or 1653 by the poet and pamphleteer, George
Wither, in a political poem entitled the " Perpetual
Parliament." His scheme was to divide the country
into twelve political units with an annual election of
one-twelfth of the total number of the parliament
from one division every month. To make his perpetual
parliament workable he suggested that members should
be paid ; and to make it genuinely perpetual he proposed that it should meet on the Sabbath as on any
other day of the week, according to the Venetian
precedent. Besides thus securing continuity, he claimed
that the constant influx of new material would make
the formation of groups and the hatching of faction
extremely difficult. Furthermore he forbade tenure of
office for two consecutive terms, upholding the democratic theory that as many people as possible should
have the opportunity of holding a responsible position.

The fourth device, by which laws were proposed
and passed by different bodies and the functions of
debating and voting were kept separate, had been
common in classical times. It had also been tried
in various republics on the continent where debating
was not taken very seriously and arguments commonly
had little effect on the decisions that were reached.
At Florence the Guelfs had for a time evolved a constitution, in which there were separate councils for
discussing and making laws.[1] At Venice, Bern,
Geneva and many Dutch cities the popular assembly

[1] *Cf.* Machiavelli, " Works," p. 27.

did little but ratify proposals submitted to it by some deliberative council, and it was often only summoned on important occasions. The same idea occurred in ecclesiastical politics. Anti-episcopalians held that two separate processes were necessary for the election of a minister, discussion by the elders and ratification of their decision by the congregation. It does not matter whether the people were supposed to have the complete power of decision, as in the theory of the Independents, or merely " the liberty of consent," as with the Presbyterians.[1]   In both cases there was the same sort of referendum.   And even in the election of the Lord Mayor of London and in the elections of those companies where officers were elected " in the presence of " the assembled members, although no actual chance of dissent was given, the same idea is present.[2]

Logically the device is based on the principle that debating and voting are different functions in the same way as making, executing, and interpreting laws. Historically it is also an intermediate stage in the struggle for popular government.   An assembly without the power to initiate legislation exists in a period when the people have won the right to give their approval or disapproval to the proposals of their rulers, whether elected or not.   The next step is the acquisition of a more positive power.

Although the idea had been previously associated with the government of small bodies of men, Harrington adopted it and extended it to the national system.   By applying it in a more radical and extreme form than had yet been known he may be said to have made it a new and different idea.   And he may stand as the

[1] *Cf.* Gillespie, " A treatise of miscellany questions," etc., 1649.   E. 564.
[2] Causton, " Elections in the City of London," clxxviii.

real author of a contrivance that appeared again in France at the time of the Revolution.

The four devices which have been considered were all practised in some form or other in various comparatively small organisations. Bodies that are aristocratic in spirit are generally organised on republican lines, and if they are not large they harbour many democratic ideas. The most exclusive London clubs, for instance, recognise the popular principle of self-government. To develop some of these ideas on a larger scale was Harrington's contribution to political thought. The growth of the national form of democracy has been in many ways automatic and independent of its other forms ; but in Harrington, who was undoubtedly one of the great democratic writers of the seventeenth century, its connection with these other channels is illustrated in a striking manner.

The use of these four contrivances, as well as the central ideas of Harrington's system, will best be realised by an analysis of the whole electoral and parliamentary system of " Oceana."

It was based in the first place on a redivision of England. Adopting the decimal system, which is associated with other revolutions, Harrington proposed to divide the country into fifty tribes approximately equal, with twenty hundreds in each tribe and ten parishes in each hundred.[1] The arrangement is based on the estimate that England and Wales contain about ten thousand parishes, which are con-

---

[1] *Cf* " A System of Politics," p. 502 : " Precincts in regulated Monarchy, where the Lords or Nobility as to their Titles or Estates ought not to be equal, but to differ as one Star differs from another in Glory, are commonly called *Countys* and ought to be inequal. Precincts in Democracy, where without equality in the Electors there will hardly be any equality in the Elected ; or where without Equality in the Precincts, it is almost, if not altogether impossible there should be equality in the Commonwealth, are properly called Tribes, and ought by all means to be equal."

venient units on which to work.[1]   The hundred was
used purely for local government.   The parishes and
tribes were the new divisions to be used instead of
the counties and boroughs in parliamentary elections.
Elections were to be in two stages.   The first stage
was the election of one-fifth of the total voting strength
of each parish to act as an electoral college for the
whole tribe.   The second stage, enacted at the chief
city of each tribe at which the delegates assembled,
was the election of the actual representatives for the
national parliament.   Clear majorities were necessary
at both stages and voting was to be secret ; nominations were to be made by committees selected by lot
for the purpose.

The need for some reform in electoral methods was
obvious.   The disorder and corruption prevalent in
parliamentary elections was enough to disgust most
serious people.   Baxter spoke with satirical eloquence
of our popular parliaments " fetched from the dung-
cart to make us laws and the May-pole to dispose of
our religion, lives and estates." [2]   Milton looked with
sorrow on the prevalence with which those who gave
the most lavish feasts and enabled the people to drink
to the greatest excess succeeded in winning elections.[3]
And a republican pamphlet summed up the situation
in these words :   " The elections of Parliament-men
are at present managed with so much tumult and
noise, that the more sober and modest people are
ashamed, and discouraged to be present at them . . .
being (as commonly managed) more like an assembly
met to chose the Lord of a Whitsun-Ale than Knights
of the Shire." [4]

[1] Graunt, in the " Observations upon the bills of Mortality," printed in
Petty's " Works," ed. Hull, ii. 372, makes the same estimate.
[2] " Holy Commonwealth," p. 229.   [3] " Prose Works," ed. 1848, i. 297.
[4] " A modest plea for an equal Commonwealth against Monarchy," p. 88.

The remedies offered by Harrington were the ballot and indirect election. He proposed and defended them on the ground that " the purity of the suffrage in a Popular Government is the health if not the life of it," [1] and " the election or suffrage of the People is most free, where it is made or given in such a manner that it can neither oblige nor disoblige another ; nor thro' fear of an Enemy or bashfulness towards a Friend, impair a man's liberty." [2] But to ensure against the possibility of corruption or demagogy, Harrington supplemented them by an elaborate system of qualifications for electors and candidates alike. He had little sympathy with the moral qualifications which were inserted in nearly all the proposals of his age. A measure like the Scotch Act of Classes of 1649, which disenfranchised all those " given to uncleanness, bribery, swearing, drunkenness or deceiving or . . . otherwise scandalous in their conversation or who neglect the worship of God in their families " was odious to him.[3] And the Instrument of Govenment with its somewhat blunt clause, " The persons who shall be elected to serve in Parliament shall be such (and no other than such) as are persons of known integrity, fearing God, and of good conversation and being of the age of twenty-one years," seemed to him an incentive to hypocrisy. The qualifications which he imposed upon electors were merely qualifications of age and sex, but those imposed on candidates were far more stringent. A candidate for the senate before passing through the ordeal of being approved by his parish, chosen by a committee selected by lot to make nominations, and elected with a clear majority by the deputies from all the

[1] " Oceana," p. 120.   [2] Ibid. p. 54.   Cf. Raleigh, " Works," viii. 29.
[3] Cf. Gardiner, " History of the Commonwealth and Protectorate," i. 161

parishes in his tribe, had to be a man of thirty years of age who had undergone military service, married, and become the owner of land, goods, or money of the value of £100. In the case of the lower house the property qualification applied only to three-sevenths of the total number, so that with the remainder comparatively poor men, Harrington claimed that, at the same time as avoiding the pitfalls of demagogy, he was remaining true to the democratic ideal and adding a new meaning to the well-worn formula, " Constitutiones et leges, quas vulgus elegerit."

Parliament, which was to be elected on this some- what complicated system, was to consist of a senate of 300 members, who would be more or less wealthy, and an assembly of 1050 which, unlike any other that had been created or suggested, seemed to Harrington to be large enough to be called representative of the people. The system of rotation, which was to secure continuity and prevent the risk of oppression attendant on long tenure of power, was to be achieved by annual elections to triennial offices. That is to say one-third of the members were automatically to retire each year, so that parliament would always have some members of two years' standing, some of one year, and some novices ; " having at once Blossoms, Fruit half-ripe, and others dropping off in full Maturity," it would "resemble an Orange-tree, such as is at the same time an Education or Spring, and a Harvest too." [1] To prevent a repetition of the scandal of the Long Parliament, which, after meeting in 1640, had passed an Act to prevent dissolution without its own consent and lived to exercise a futile government over a country which it could no longer claim to represent till it was ejected in 1653 by Oliver Cromwell's

[1] " Oceana," p. 140.

strong arm, Harrington declared members ineligible for two consecutive terms.

In making provision against what Shakespeare called " the insolence of office," he was voicing a widely felt sentiment. Winstanley had observed, " if water stands long it corrupts. . . . Some officers of the Commonwealth have grown so mossy for want of removing that they will hardly speak to an old acquaintance." [1] Nedham used language of much the same strain. " When it happens that a supreme power long continues in the hands of any person or persons ; they, by greatness of place being seated above the middle region of the people, sit secure from all winds and weathers, and from those storms of violence that nip and terrify the inferior part of the world ; whereas if by a successive revolution of authority, they came to be degraded by their earthly godheads, and return into the same condition with other mortals, they must needs be the most sensible and tender of what shall be laid upon them." [2] And the same idea had been thus expressed in verse by Wither.

> " By *these means* they, who do command to-day,
> Shall learn again *to-morrow* to obey.
> Many shall be encouraged to enable
> Themselves in public to be serviceable ;
> And in few years some thousand more than now,
> The *common interest* shall learn to know ;
> And how they may advance it, when they come
> From that *Grand School* to live again at home ;
> And, think themselves, obliged and ev'rywhere,
> To further it as well as sitting there."

The scheme of rotation, compared by Harrington

---

[1] " The Law of Freedom in a Platform," p. 27.

[2] " Excellencie of a Free State," p. 36. For a modern psychological defence of rotation, based on the argument that the normal man requires a combination of publicity and privacy, see Graham Wallas, " Human Nature in Politics," p. 53.

in a brilliant passage to the natural provision for the
alternation of day and night,[1] was of course open to
criticism.   But he was justified in pointing out that a
political experience of three years in a parliament
always in session was equal to twenty years in one
that was hardly ever sitting.[2]   In a modern community
of business men the best people would be unwilling
to submit to the interruptions necessitated by the
sacrifice of alternate periods of their life to public
service.   But in a country of landed gentry like that
which Harrington had in mind, the plough and the
sword are not incompatible.[3]   Whatever is said of this
portion of Harrington's scheme, he must be given
credit for a certain sanity and moderation.   He did
not adopt the Roman consular system in all its severity,
but permitted re-election to office after the lapse of
a single term.   To induce all classes to come forward
he supported the payment of members.   He attempted
to combine the two opposing ideals of democracy—
the glorification of average ability, and the advance-
ment of merit, in whatever class it shows itself.   By
multiplying the number of offices and making vacations
compulsory he ensured a certain amount of executive
power to the ordinary man ;   by permitting future
re-election he provided for the retention of all who
displayed ability in their first term of office.

The most important of all the provisions for the
prevention of demagogy is found in the functions
assigned to the two chambers.   The titles, Senate
and Prerogative Tribe, show that Harrington was
thinking primarily of the ancient city state.   The
problem which he undertook was to fit the contrivances

---

[1] " Oceana," p. 56.   [2] " Valerius and Publicola," p. 484.
[3] This was shown very emphatically in some of the American colonies
during the seventeenth century.

of the classical age into the representative parliamentary system.   Bearing in his mind the image of
the Athenian ἐκκλήσια, which had degenerated into
anarchy as soon as debating had been introduced,
he separated what he termed the functions of debate
and result, giving the former to the Senate and the
latter to the Assembly.   The greatest order was to be
observed in the debates of the Senate.   All business
was to be introduced by a magistrate, and in the
subsequent debate priority was to be given to senior
members.   At the conclusion of the debate the motion
was to be put to the ballot.   Alternatives to the
official proposal were also to be submitted, and those
that received the least support were to be ruled out
until a clear majority could be obtained.   A proposal
which obtained this clear majority was termed a decree
of the Senate.   A decree, though of itself invalid, was
capable of being referred by one of the magistrates
to the Prerogative Tribe, which was properly the
legislative organ.   This body, after listening to the
arguments on both sides of the question, which were
laid before them by senators picked for the purpose,
proceeded to the ballot without debating, and either
rejected or passed into law the proposals that were
referred to them.

It is noticeable in this connection that Harrington
did not confine the use of the ballot to the election of
members.   Believing as he did in the wisdom of
members, who would be elected by his elaborate
system, he left them in entire liberty to act according
to their own principles, and by the introduction of
the ballot into the house itself he ensured that the
way they voted should be unknown even to the constituency which they represented.   He was consistent.
For the ideas of systems of double election and large

electoral divisions are both based on the theory that
a representative does not bear a mandate from his
constituency, but is nothing more than a man, in
whose personal judgment and discretion his people
are willing to place confidence. This is not the democratic theory, but it is the theory on which the parliamentary representation of England, even at the time
of its greatest corruption, was founded. It is only in
very recent times that the alternative theory has found
support in the country; and the deadening rigour of
party discipline, which accompanies it, might itself
be checked by introducing the secret voting of Oceana
into the modern House of Commons.

Harrington's reason for desiring the double-
chamber system was illustrated in a homely little
simile, which deserves mention because it shows that
in spite of his historical method Harrington was not
blind to the psychological approach to politics, of
which so much is heard to-day. He imagines a situation in which two girls have got a cake, "by the gift
of an Uncle or Aunt, or by purchase, or such a one
perhaps as was of their own making." For the sake
of the political comparison the two girls must be supposed to want to secure as much of it as they can. The
only way this cake can be fairly divided, says Harrington, is for one to cut it and the other to have the
first choice. The girl who cuts the cake, wanting as
large a piece as possible, but knowing that she is not
going to have the selection, will naturally divide it
equally, so that she may have at any rate one half. If
she also had the first choice, she might cut it differ-
ently. On the other hand, if they merely sit and dispute
about it, in steps some rude fellow, who takes it and
eats it—by Divine Right—(the prettiest touch of all).[1]

[1] "Oceana," pp. 47-8. "Prerogative of Popular Government," pp. 252, 256.

The necessity for assigning his two chambers separate functions was shown in four aphorisms :

" The Reason of the Senat is, that a Popular Assembly rightly constituted is not capable of any prudent debate."

" The Reason of the Popular Assembly is, that a Senat rightly constituted for Debate, must consist of so few and eminent persons, that if they have the Result too, they will not resolve according to the Interest of the people, but according to the Interest of themselves."

" A Popular Assembly without a Senat cannot be wise."

" A Senat without a Popular Assembly will not be honest." [1]

In other words, realising the perils of eloquence which beset the democratic state, believing in the system of checks and balances, and holding that there is an important distinction between the capacity for " invention," and the capacity for " judgment," Harrington was induced to separate the functions of debate and result, just as he separated the legislative, executive, and judiciary.

But further considerations were in his mind. He was in the first place consciously aiming at a species of referendum. He later described the assembly as " nothing else but an instrument or method whereby to receive the result of the whole nation with order and expedition and without any manner of tumult and confusion." [2] A direct appeal to the people, which would have been a clumsy procedure in the seventeenth century when communication was difficult,

---

[1] " Political Aphorisms," Nos. 74-77, p. 519.
[2] " Valerius and Publicola," p. 491. *Cf.* " Oceana," p. 48. " A whole nation is too unwieldy a body to be assembled."

would satisfy Harrington no more than direct popular elections. If they produced a sense of responsibility they would produce disorder. He therefore preferred to give to an elective body the duty of weighing every argument calmly, and estimating the opinion of the country, and made the curious suggestion of what may be termed an indirect referendum or a referendum to a representative body.

In the second place his scheme seemed a not unattractive solution to the much-vexed question of the relation of the two Houses of Parliament. There was an admirable simplicity in letting one house debate and the other vote. But it is questionable if the requisite purpose would be achieved. One of two things might be expected. As the two chambers were composed largely of classes of the same social and economic standing, they would either work together with a dangerous unity of purpose and entirely cease to act as checks on one another, or else there would be constant deadlock between the two houses ; for the one method of asserting any genuine power, which the assembly possessed, was the refusal to give their assent ; an affirmative acquiescence in the proposals of the Senate meant a powerless inactivity.

It is true that the two theories of the democratic ideal are again combined. Ability is intended to find its way into the upper house, while the ordinary man exercises the sovereign legislative power in the lower house. And as the members of the latter are meant to represent or follow public opinion, not to educate it, there is no need for them to debate. It is, however, equally true that the upper house would have no sense of responsibility, and the lower house, voting as it did in darkness, would have no incentive to exercise care or judgment in forming their opinions.

This separation of debate and result, proposing and passing laws, is not without interest to the political student of to-day, who is watching the development of a somewhat similar process. Modern experience is daily showing the convenience of curtailing as far as possible opportunities to propose or even to discuss bills. The initiation of legislation and the major part of the subsequent discussion is accordingly being left to Cabinet Ministers, and the private member is becoming little more than a machine, whose function is to register a silent vote as his party dictates. It need therefore cause little surprise if the process is extended a step further, to culminate in the introduction of a referendum, which will separate the functions of debate and result in a more obvious manner.

The whole scheme may be summed up in a few words. Wishing to avoid the faults of the old system and the excesses of the new republicanism, Harrington selected the four contrivances which have been emphasised. The movement which he started was almost new to national politics. It has since been discovered that the indirect method of election breeds corruption in spite of its theoretical advantages. But the ballot is now one of the keystones of democracy; rotation has become a part of the normal machinery in the organisation of the modern upper chamber; the indirect referendum has been reproduced without very great differences in the present relation between the Cabinet and the House of Commons. Yet Harrington was the only writer of his age who clearly saw the advantages of these municipal devices. It is hard to say how far he realised the democratic value of the system of checks and balances. At one time he seems to hold that friction and delay, by bringing to light the small considerations which really

supply the key to disputed questions and by giving
public opinion the chance to assert itself, produce a
form of democracy which is in a sense more democratic
than the direct form.   At another time his motives
seem to be aristocratic.   For he had seen under direct
democracy flagrant disorder and oppression comparable with the oppression of a monarch ; and he hoped
by mechanical devices to prevent its repetition.   Whatever his exact position may have been, he hoped to
contrive a moderate democracy of a permanent nature
by reforming the land system and the electoral and
parliamentary procedure.

§ 3

In addition to his agrarian law and the other
measures which have been referred to, many interesting
ideas and suggestions are to be found in Harrington's
writings.

In an age which thought and fought about theology
and a revolution which found its inspiration in the
Puritan ideal, religious questions played a more
active part in the political life of England than they
had ever done before or have done since.   The change
from Erastianism to theocracy and the rise of sectarian-
ism had produced a sudden shock throughout the
length and breadth of the country.   Complete religious
liberty was in a moment won by all sections of the
Puritan party, and the disorder which ensued produced
an equally disordered mass of suggestions for the
religious settlement of the nation.   There were, however, three main policies which were proposed.   (i) Absolute liberty of conscience and no national church
or state-interference with religion of any kind whatso-
ever.   (ii) Unlimited toleration round an established

national church.   (iii) A limited toleration round an
etablished national church.[1]   Harrington, who was
never an extremist, ranged himself with those who, like
Cromwell and the framers of the Instrument of Government, held the third of these views.

The point in common between the three was the
recognition of the existence of dissent. The idea of
compelling absolute uniformity in doctrine was given
up. Toleration became the orthodox theory, supported with a certain monotony on all sides by arguments based on the nature of religon. Harrington
showed no originality in advocating toleration ; but
the point of view which he took was entirely his own.
He seized upon a fact, which in the broadest terms
was as undisputed as the connection of power and
property, and applied it in exactly the same way.
The connection of the democratic movements in
Church and State was obvious to Hobbes and must
have been realised by most people, who had lived
through the latter part of Charles I.'s reign. But
before Harrington wrote " Oceana," no one had thought
of drawing up a systematic account of it, and no one
was able to use with any confidence the argument
that toleration is the natural complement of democracy.
Harrington's theory made this possible, and drew
the question from the region of rights to that of
facts, His theory that " Without Liberty of Conscience,
Civil Liberty cannot be perfect ; and without Civil
Liberty, Liberty of Conscience cannot be perfect," [2]
was repeated in varying strains in all his works. But
the most complete discussion was given in his admirable summary in the " System of Politics," [3] where, by

---

[1] This analysis is given in Masson, " Life of Milton," ii. 122-29. Although
Masson refers particularly to the year 1645, the division may be applied to the
whole period.

[2] " Valerius and Publicola," p. 489.   [3] " A System of Politics," pp. 505-8.

considering the conditions of religion under monarchy, regulated monarchy and democracy, he brought out exactly what he meant by this connection. In an absolute monarchy like that of the Turk, where the civil power is vested in the hands of a single person, it had been shown to be possible to permit a certain amount of religious liberty, because without political liberty it is not dangerous. In a regulated monarchy like that of England toleration is not safe (though perhaps inevitable), because when it comes, it means the abolition of the episcopacy, which is " one half of the Foundations of regulated Monarchy." " Democracy being nothing but intire Liberty ; and Liberty of Conscience without Civil Liberty or Civil Liberty without Liberty of Conscience being but Liberty by halves, must admit of Liberty of Conscience both as to the perfection of its present being, and as to its future security ; as to the perfection of its present being, for the Reasons already shown, or that she do not injoy Liberty by halves ; and for the future security, because this excludes Absolute Monarchy, which cannot stand with Liberty of Conscience in the whole, and Regulated Monarchy, which cannot stand safely with it in any part." [1]

This theory, though not universally valid, has been called one of the great discoveries of the seventeenth century. It served as a new argument both for republicanism and toleration—for the former with those more ardent Puritans who subordinated political to religious motives, for the latter with men like Harrington himself, who was primarily a republican.

In spite of his general belief in toleration and his realisation of its inevitability, he did not accept it in its completest form. He always feared extreme

[1] " A System of Politics," p. 506.

measures. He therefore did not follow the large
section of Puritans who refused to grant religious
liberty to Anglicanism. But on political grounds he
excluded Jews, Papists and idolaters from toleration—
Jews because they never mixed with nations that gave
them protection, Papists because they owed allegiance
to a foreign potentate, idolaters because, like Robespierre, he believed in the supreme necessity of religion
for securing social order. To all other religious bodies
he proposed to give complete toleration.

But in rejecting the extreme position Harrington
went further than this. The argument for religious
liberty is not without its complications, but it may
be generally resolved into the argument for individualism. However admirable individualism is as an ideal,
it is in fact controverted by two tendencies in human
nature—the tendency to follow the majority and the
tendency to seek the advice of the expert. This was
realised in full by the most thorough-going individual-
ists, and they attempted to defeat it by abolishing
the national church as well as weakening the power of
the priest. Harrington, however, was a man of more
moderate views. He was aware that people, as a matter
of fact, do not make up their own minds on matters
of religion but either " engage to believe no otherwise
than is believed by my Lord Bishop or goodman
Presbyter," [1] or follow blindly the lead of the majority,[2]
and he trusted the instincts of the people more than
the advice of the priest ; furthermore he believed that
there is a national conscience no less than an individual
conscience to which liberty is due.[3] He therefore
retained the idea of a State Church, and he saw no

[1] " Oceana," p. 59.

[2] "The major part of Mankind gives itself up in the matter of Religion
to the public leading" ("Political Aphorism," No. 39, p. 517)

[3] "Oceana," p. 58.

more objection to its public endowment than to the payment of members of parliament. " To hold that Hirelings (as they are term'd by some) or an indowed Ministry ought to be remov'd out of the Church," he wrote in 1659, alluding to Milton's pamphlet, " is inconsistent with a Commonwealth." [1] But to prevent the corruption which attends the acquisition of civil interest by the clergy, illustrated by the whole course of history from the occasion when the Jewish people submitted to the influence of the priesthood and raised the cry, " Crucify Him ; Crucify Him," down to the latest intrigue of the Pope, he proposed to restrict their power. Following the example of Venice, where the clergy were ineligible for secular offices,[2] and the Netherlands, where a pair of shoes used to be sent as a gentle hint to the minister that meddled in politics,[3] Harrington proposed to make it illegal for preachers to sit in parliament. This had already been done in England itself under its republican form of government, and it was in close accord with Harrington's general views on the separation of powers.

The State Church, which he proposed, differed considerably from the organisation which the Puritans had overthrown. He realised, as few others of his time did, that the politician is wise to keep clear of doctrine, and made no attempt to supply his Church with a creed, or state what sects it would be able to embrace. He merely made provisions for its material welfare. In the hope of encouraging better men to come forward, he proposed to increase all stipends and to make the ministry, like all other offices, elective. Candidates were to be sent to the various parishes for

[1] "Political Aphorisms," p. 516.
[2] See the approbation of this measure in Thuanus, Lib. 23. " Interdicti Veneti Historia," Lib. i. Raleigh. " Works," vii. 44.
[3] " Oceana," p. 181.

one year on probation. At the end of this time a
ballot was to be taken, at which they would require a
two-third's majority in their congregations to be
elected. He felt, however, that there was a certain
risk in thus democratising the Church, and hoped to
counteract it by making a university education a
necessary qualification for the ministry. Milton had
protested against this ; [1] the Quakers also held that
" being bred at Oxford or Cambridge is not enough to
fit or qualify men to be ministers of Christ " ; and the
following stanza from a contemporary song shows that
the prevalent practice was not held in great respect :

> " Oxford and Cambridge make poor preachers,
> Each shop affordeth better teachers,
> Oh, blessed Reformation." [2]

But Harrington with his fear of demagogy, his interest
in scholarship, and his conviction that the purity of
religion depends largely on the correct translation of
the Bible adhered to his point.[3] And he further
hoped to prevent disorder by the establishment of an
elective national Council of Religion to which dissenters
as well as members of the State Church were invited
to refer disputes.

After religion, military problems must have seemed
of greater importance than anything else to the age
which we are discussing. England possessed a large
standing army for the first time in its history, and was
virtually governed by its greatest general, Oliver
Cromwell. Discontent at the military régime was
rife, and cries for the disbanding of the army were
widespread. Harrington, remembering the history of
Rome and the double functions of her greatest magistrates, the consul, the prætor, and the tribune, did

[1] Masson, v. 614.
[2] Percy Soc. Publications, " Political Ballads of the Commonwealth," III. ii.
[3] " Oceana," p. 179.

not share in the general feelings of disgust at the confusion of civil and military power, but nevertheless he proposed measures framed to prevent its abuse.   This is the interpretation of the extraordinary proposal to extend the principles of election and rotation to the army.

The details of the system are described in a somewhat complicated manner and call for a brief summary.

What is called the first " essay " is formed by the election of one-fifth of all the youth, not destined for a commercial or professional life, in every parish. They are elected for one year, and are ineligible for a second year's service without a vacation.   They are themselves elected in the parishes, and they elect their officers at the hundreds.   The second " essay " is formed by the election out of these of 600 foot and 200 horse from each tribe.   These taken together form the standing army of 30,000 foot and 10,000 horse. If these are mobilised they become *ipso facto* the third essay, together with the armies 5000 strong in foot and 1000 in horse elected at the same time as the second out of the first essay for three years' service in Scotland and Ireland, and another second essay is elected.   Men over thirty are to be encouraged to come forward for active service as " volunteers,"[1] in which case the unfittest of the youth are to be dismissed to keep the numbers right.   In case of invasion the whole male population is expected to take arms.   The Commander-in-Chief is elected annually in Parliament.

This imitation of the military organisation of Rome, with the elective principle extended from officers to men, is one of the most interesting of Harrington's proposals.   It would not appear so

[1] " The Art of Lawgiving," p. 455.

curious to the seventeenth century as it does to the twentieth ; for the election of the constable was a common practice in the English parish, while in the Netherlands the officers of the militia were in many places chosen by the men. Nor would the compulsory periods of vacation seem so absurd. A continuous and specialised military training was not essential to the simple conditions of warfare at the time, and the problem before the country was not how to produce but how to check a successful army which had assumed civil power.

In calculating the numbers of his army, Harrington was doubtless guided to some extent by the actual size of the armed forces in Great Britain at the time. The numbers in the New Model fluctuated considerably.[1] In 1652 it had comprised some 70,000 men. But by 1654 it had been reduced to rather under 53,000 ; and Harrington, who was writing " Oceana " at about this time, was willing to accept these numbers as on the whole suitable for his new England. The idea of electing the soldiers in the counties may have been also suggested by contemporary practice. For, up to the time when the forces would be maintained at sufficient strength by voluntary enlistment, it had been the duty of the separate counties to provide the men. The quota of each country was fixed, and the men had to be found by a given date.[2] Election might well seem to Harrington a more constitutional method of supplying the army than impressment. In this problem as in all the other problems with which he dealt Harrington was willing to accept much in the existing state of things. Ancient Rome and Venice were at the back of his mind, but contemporary England was before his eyes.

[1] Firth, " Cromwell's Army," p. 35.   [2] *Ibid.* p. 36.

The attempt made by Harrington to separate civil and ecclesiastical functions and the precautions suggested against the abuse of the confusion of military and civil power lead naturally to another large question, of which they form a part. The doctrine of the separation of powers, which may be traced back to the period of the Commonwealth, was not at first restricted to the definite form, under which it was made famous by Montesquieu. It differed from it in two respects. In the first place the strict division of government into legislative, executive, and judicial functions was not universally accepted. As late as 1689 Locke wrote of legislative, judicial, and federative organs, while in our own period we find the functions of "Legislative, Judiciary, and Military Power" discussed. In the second place the terms executive and judicial had not yet come to represent two entirely different functions of government. In his " Excellence of a Free-State " Nedham spoke of the power of the judge as executive ; and a similar use of the word occurs in " Oceana " itself, where Harrington wrote : " A Commonwealth . . . must consist . . . of the three general Orders ; that is to say of the Senat debating and proposing, of the People resolving, and of the Magistracy executing. . . . The third Order is executive, to which answers that part of the same Science which is stil'd of the Frame and Course of Courts or Judicatorys." [1] But without the exactness of form which it assumed with Montesquieu, the doctrine was widely held by the supporters of the Commonwealth.

In practice the three functions of government had not been separated. The confusion of judicial and legislative functions in mediæval England has been

---

[1] " Animadversions upon General Monk's letter to the gentry of Devon," E. 1015.

brilliantly illustrated by a recent writer." [1]   The
similar confusion of judicial and executive functions
in the duties of the Council, in central government,
and the Justices of the Peace, in local government, is
too obvious to need amplification, being reflected, as
we have seen, even in political phraseology.   Protests,
however, against the prevailing practice were numerous,
and the doctrine of the separation of powers was widely
asserted.   " The reason is evident," wrote Nedham,
" because, if the Law-Makers (who ever have the
Supream Power) should be also the constant Adminis-
trators and Dispensers of Law and Justice, then (by
consequence) the people would be left without Remedy,
in case of Injustice, since no Appeal can lie under
heaven against such as have the Supremacy ; which,
if once admitted, were inconsistent with the very
interest and natural import of true Policy ; which
ever supposeth, that men in Power may be unrighteous ;
and therefore (presuming the worst) points alwayes,
in all determination, at the Enormities and Remedies
of government, on the behalf of the people." [2]   Cromwell in his speech of April 21st, 1657, burst into
sarcasm over the idea of a perpetual parliament,
beginning by appointing judicial committees and
ending (as in Naylor's case) by the assumption of
judicial powers by the whole house—" And truly I
think the Legislative would be almost as well in the
Four Courts of Westminster Hall !   And if they could
make Laws and judge too, you would have excellent
Laws ; and the lawyers would be able to give you
excellent counsel." [3]   Harrington in his epigrammatic
style expressed the same sentiment, " In a Commonwealth neither is accumulations of magistracy just or

---

[1] McIlwain, " The High Court of Parliament and its Supremacy."
[2] " Excellence of a Free State," p. 212.   [3] Carlyle, Speech XIII.

equal, nor the confounding of Executive and Legislative Magistracy safe." [1]

The measure by which he hoped to secure this was the simple and popular one of excluding practising lawyers from Parliament—in the words of one of his followers—" it being very incongruous in reason that they should be the makers of our Laws that are the mercenary Interpreters, lest byast by their own interests, instead of fences to our proprieties they make them snares to our Lives and Estates." [2]

Thus far Harrington went with the orthodox supporters of the Protectorate. But at the same time as agreeing with them he saw the force of the opposite and classical theory, " wheresoever the power of making Law is, there only is the power of interpreting the law so made." [3] This led him to make two propositions by way of exception to the Montesquieuan doctrine. He maintained that there must be an ultimate appeal to the people in their representatives so that the lower house should in the last resort exercise judicial functions. And although he acknowledged he could not understand " why a Judge, being but an Assistant or Lawyer should be Member of a Legislative Council," he felt the occasional utility of consulting the judges in framing laws. He therefore proposed that the judiciary should be elected by his system of ballot and rotation out of either house or both houses of Parliament, and that the judges should be permitted to sit in the Senate but not exercise their vote.

It is not difficult to reconcile Harrington's two positions. With the sacred example of Rome before him he could not refuse the right of appeal to the

---

[1] "The Art of Lawgiving," p. 465.
[2] " A Modest Plea for an equal Commonwealth against Monarchy," p. 73.
[3] " A System of Politics," p. 509.

people in their elected assembly. He therefore made
no attempt to bring about the absolute separation of
legislative and judicial functions. But at the same
time he felt the dangers of the concentration of power,
and he was inspired with a hatred of the legal caste.
He was therefore compelled to take certain steps against
the confusion of powers. Without making any clear
distinction between judicial and executive power, he
asserted in general terms the doctrine of the separation
of the three functions of government. But he did not
believe that the separation of the making, administering,
and interpreting of laws was so great a preservative
of liberty as to stand in no need of qualification. In
his petition of July 6th 1659 he therefore tabulated
his attitude thus : " That it ought to be declar'd as a
Fundamental Order in the Constitution of this Commonwealth, that the Parliament being the Supreme Legislative Power, is intended only for the exercise of all
those Acts of Authority that are proper and peculiar to the Legislative Power ; and to provide for a
Magistracy to whom should appertain the whole
Executive Power of the Laws : and no Case, either
Civil or Criminal, to be judged in Parliament, saving
that the last Appeals in all Cases, where Appeals shall
be thought fit to be admitted, be only to the Popular
Assembly ; and also that to them be refer'd the
Judgment of all Magistrates in Cases of Maladministra-
tion in their offices."

Harrington's views on the relations of states with
each other are worthy of mention. He accepted
Machiavelli's division of states and foreshadowed the
modern classification of unitary and federal, national
and imperial states,[1] although in 1659 he relegated
federal systems from the domain of art to that of

[1] " Oceana," p. 54.

chance.[1] His views on the proper treatment of
Scotland and Ireland were somewhat unsettled. He
first proposed that the neighbouring countries should
be represented in Parliament, but be governed by
Councils of State, elected from retiring senators, with
the assistance of the provincial armies. But when
the question of the representation of Scotland and
Ireland came up in Parliament in 1659, Nevile opposed
the motion, and the common attitude of the republican
members is represented in the words of one of their
number—" I think it is best that they should have
Parliaments of their own for that very reason, that
votes may not be imposed upon you here. There is
a sea between us and Dublin." [2] Similarly Harrington,
when he wrote the " Political Aphorisms " in August
1659 deplored a union, which could only be based on
force, and claimed nothing but " a just league,"
which would leave to Scotland and Ireland their own
laws, their own government, and their perfect liberty.[3]

In his random remarks on the colonial system
Harrington sounds extraordinarily modern. He has
been greeted by some as one of the first of British
Imperialists ; and Froude has given the title " Oceana "
to his book on the British Empire in Harrington's
honour. But outside of the Preface to " Oceana,"
where England is assigned an imperial position more
proud than that of Venice, a different strain is heard.
" If you have subdued a nation that is capable of
Liberty, you shall make them a present of it," he says
in one place,[4] while in another place the following
famous passage occurs : " The colonys in the Indies
they are yet babes that cannot live without sucking
the breasts of their Mother Citys, but such as I mistake,

[1] " A System of Politics," p. 502.   [2] Burton, " Diary," iii. 238.
[3] " Political Aphorisms," p. 518.   [4] 'Oceana," p. 201.

if when they come of age they do not wean themselves, which causes me to wonder at Princes that delight to be exhausted in that way." [1]   This was written in 1656.   No wonder Harrington has influenced American thought !

The author of " Oceana " was never quite comfortable about imperialism.   He felt that it contradicted his theory of the balance of property.   Nevertheless his prophecy of the American Revolution was in reality based on the theory.   " Provincial or dependent Empire," he argued, "is not to be exercised by them that have the balance of dominion in the province [*i.e.* the landowners], because they would bring the government from provincial and dependent to national and independent." [2]   In other words a national sentiment is bound to arise, if a colony is allowed to govern itself. In view, then, of the liberal policy of the mother country to her colonies, Harrington was able to predict the assertion of their independence, and his prediction was based on the idea that the landowners will always rule where they have the chance.

In common with his Hellenic models Harrington laid great stress on education.   The theory that " the Education of a man's own children is not wholly to be committed or trusted to himself " [3] is as ancient as it is modern.   But Harrington's application of the theory is more suggestive of the spirit of the nineteenth century than of the stern régime of Sparta or the Roman Republic.   He proposed the institution of compulsory free schools under government inspection, but with his usual moderation he left the education of only sons to the discretion of their parents and gave all parents the liberty of choosing the schools to which they sent their children.   The absence of any allusion

---

[1] " Oceana," p. 44.   [2] *Ibid.* p. 43.   [3] *Ibid.* p. 172.

to the education of girls is not remarkable. Women played an extraordinarily small part in the revolutionary movement in England. And the classical enthusiasts could find very few examples of women who had played a great part in ancient history. As Algernon Sidney said, " No man ever heard of a Queen, or a man deriving his title from a female among the ancient civilisations. . . . When God describes who should be the King of his people (if they have one) and how he should govern ; no mention is made of daughters." [1] Consequently the only functions which Harrington assigns to women are those of squabbling over a piece of cake, and making linen pellets inscribed with " Aye " or " No " for the use of their husbands or brothers at the tribal elections.[2]

The part which universities were intended to play in the religious life of " Oceana " has already been described. In its secular life their position was less emphasised, though Harrington was conscious of the debt which he himself owed to his university education.[3] Many proposed their abolition ; all proposed to reform them. Harrington himself constantly referred to the " reformed universities " of Oceana, but he never tabulated any scheme. However there is little doubt that the scheme proposed in the " Modest Plea for an Equal Commonwealth against Monarchy," a pamphlet which in all other respects reflects Harrington's ideas closely, is substantially what the Harringtonians desired. The writer first attacked the system of government at the university—the unlimited power in the hands of the Heads of Houses, " those little living idols or Monuments of Monarchy," and the common

---

[1] Sidney, " Discourses on Government," p. 47.
[2] In the census which he desired the female population was to be neglected (" Oceana," p. 97).   [3] " The Art of Lawgiving," p. 427.

practice of arranging the elections of the fellows, then the scholastic and monkish atmosphere in which studies are pursued, and finally submitted his scheme. He proposed in the first place to scatter the colleges about the country, and in the second place entirely to alter the course of studies, introducing modern languages, law, agriculture, economics, chemistry, art, English, military studies, dancing, fencing and (lastly) travel, in the hopes of making "learning more pleasant and acceptable to gentlemen" and "stocking the Nation with a more able and learned gentry for the service of the Commonwealth than heretofore it hath been."[1]   The value of continental travel was one of Harrington's most constant themes ; and in his own remarks on education he added a proposal to encourage students to follow his own example and write books on the constitutions of the countries which they visited, to be published, if meritorious, by the state.

But a university career was not the normal course for the young men of Oceana. After leaving school at eighteen, those who were destined for public life would naturally undergo without delay the military training, which was, except in the case of only children, one of the qualifications for magistracy.

The political education of the people was to continue in an institution called the Academy, which was adapted from an organisation, which Harrington had often seen stimulating literary activity in the cities of Italy. It was to consist of an informal meeting held every evening and open to all who wished to supply the government with information or take part in discussions on political questions. Besides educating the people it was intended to give the govern-

[1] "Modest Plea for an equal Commonwealth against Monarchy," pp. 45-55.

ment an opportunity of keeping in touch with the
country and helping to form public opinion.   The enforced silence of the lower house in Oceana would rather
suggest that Harrington failed to realise the political
value of debating.   This institution, however, together
with the systematic public speaking, " The Tuesday
lectures or orations to the people," which he proposes
elsewhere,[1] show that no less than his counterpart in
the French Revolution, the Abbé Sieyès, he felt that
without perpetual discussion it is almost impossible to
produce that public opinion on which all democratic
governments must rest.

The institution of the four Councils of State, Trade,
Religion, and War is interesting, but more important
is the proposed transplantation of nearly all the
Roman magistracies to England.   The consular
system is reproduced by the Lord Strategus, who is
Commander-in-Chief of the army as well as President
of the Senate, and the Lord Orator, who, as his name
implies, is a glorified Speaker.   " Oceana " has its
censors, who are entrusted with the supervision of the
national religion and the maintenance of the purity of
the suffrage, and who are at the same time *ex-officio*
Chancellors of the two great universities, its Tribunes,
who are of little importance, and finally its Dictator.
In times of emergency the Senate may elect nine new
members to the Council of War and declare this en-
larged body Dictator of Oceana, with power to levy
men, declare war, and make what laws it wishes.
Its existence is limited to three months, and the laws
that it makes become invalid at the end of a year
unless they are ratified in the usual way by the Senate
and the people.

The Council of War itself is given the very important

[1] " Oceana," pp. 157 and 160.

duty of acting like the Spartan ephorate as the guardian
of the constitution, and declaring void all measures
that are contrary to its fundamental provisions. We
shall notice later what emphasis Harrington laid on
this idea.

It is impossible to do more than notice a few of the
miscellaneous suggestions offered in " Oceana," many
of them seeming to sound a modern note. Under the
inspiration of the Athenian ideal and the Italian
Renaissance, the capital city is to be beautified ; public
parks and buildings are to be preserved ; a national
theatre is to be built.[1] The elective principle is to be
so far extended as to include even the poet laureate,
who is to be elected with a two-thirds majority by
the Academy.[2] In accord with the Utopian tradition,
marriage is not neglected by the state. But Oceana is
to have nothing so radical as the ideal states of More or
Plato had. Harrington is satisfied by converting the
ceremony into a civil rite, by making marriage a qualification for office, by taxing bachelors, and by allowing
abatements for every child. At the same time he de-
plores marrying for money and suggests a limitation of
dowries. A census of the population is to be taken,
but it is to be confined to adult males. The continuation of the payment of members and the schemes
for compulsory free education and land valuation have
already been alluded to.

These miscellaneous suggestions in " Oceana " must
lead us once more to the classical learning with which
Harrington's work is so saturated. Although much
of "Oceana" is Jewish, Venetian, or English, much more
of it is Greek and Roman. Harrington was essentially
a child of the Renaissance, one who desired to introduce the politics of the city states of antiquity into

[1] " Oceana," p. 168.   [2] *Ibid.* p. 223.

England. He looked chiefly to the constitutions of Sparta, Athens, and Rome; but there was another constitution, made for an imaginary colony in Crete, to which he also turned. Harrington never mentions Plato's " Laws," but it is difficult not to believe that he was influenced by the second best republic of the Greek philosopher. It is, like Oceana, a practical sort of Utopia, almost an expanded written constitution. In spirit the two works are strikingly similar, and the resemblance extends to detailed proposals. The Cretan colony which Plato is to found is to start with the dictatorship of a single individual, a legislator, who is to produce laws which will be so good that the people will be happy to live under their rule, and the state will last for ever. By regulating property and establishing a system of checks and balances the equilibrium will be maintained, but guardians of the constitution will be appointed as an additional security. Debating will apparently be forbidden in the assembly. The election of the council will be made indirectly, with a mixture of lot and election, and written votes will be used. In the army, officers will be elected by the men. There are many other small suggestions which appear again in " Oceana " ; and in particular the value of foreign travel is recognised in a similar but less liberal fashion.

" Oceana " is no mere reproduction of " The Laws," as many of these points appear in a very different setting in Harrington's work, and some (such as the enforced silence of the assembly) which Plato scarcely mentions are treated with the greatest emphasis. But there can be little doubt that Harrington was influenced by the work of Plato's old age, and that " The Laws " occupied an important position in the classical background to " Oceana."

Enough has been said of Harrington's work to show that he was no revolutionary demagogue. In the history of English political thought he must be placed as the forerunner of Locke and of the individualist utilitarians of the eighteenth and nineteenth centuries. The following sentence, taken from his " System of Politics," might have served as a motto for the doctrines of the latter, " The interest of Democracy is the felicity of the people : for in Democracy the government is for the use of the people." [1] He was a writer of restraint, who rarely allowed himself to stray on to the psychological aspect of the democratic ideal, but here and there he produced sentences and sentiments worthy of Abraham Lincoln. " Whereas the People taken apart are but so many privat interests but if you take them together they are the public interest." [2] " The people cannot see but they can feel." [3] These are the very catchwords of modern democracy. But Harrington rarely let them fall. He preferred to confine the main part of his work to a concrete illustration or a historical defence of the principles which he held. He believed that there was no such thing as pure democracy except at the moments of a nation's history, when the people, " reduced to misery and despair become their own Politicians, as certain Beasts, when they are sick, become their own Physicians." [4] The true ideal of democracy is not attained when the people take the government into their own hands, but when with aconscious exercise of their sovereign power (they cannot, as Hobbes would have them, resign it [5]) they content themselves with electing representatives to adopt or reject the proposals made by others of their own number.

[1] " A System of Politics," p. 501.   [2] "Oceana," p. 155.
[3] " Political Aphorisms," p. 515.   [4] "Oceana," p. 151.
                    [5] Valerius and Publicola," p. 478.

CHAPTER IV

Harrington's Public Life and Minor Writings

Harrington's work, which had at first been regarded as dangerous, was very soon labelled as too unpractical to call for any alarm. The following which the isolated and unknown author gathered round him was at first not considerable. He could hardly have hoped to win favour with the so-called republicans. The party was itself not united. The Fifth Monarchy men, who were in favour of adopting the republican form of government till Christ returned to occupy the throne, were still active. Harrington called them hypocrites. The other section, led by men like Ludlow and Haselrigge, were entirely out of touch with them; they protested against the monarchical element in the Protectorate, because they desired to return to the form of parliamentary government which had been exercised by the Long Parliament from 1649 to 1653. Harrington called them oligarchists. If he received little support from the party which stood for republican institutions, he must have expected still less sympathy from the supporters of the government of the Protector.

Cromwell read " Oceana " and laughed at it, remarking in his dry manner that " the Gentleman had like to trepan him out of his Power, but that what he got by the Sword he would not quit for a little paper shot." [1] But he did not despise Harrington. He

---

[1] Toland, xx.

realised that there was a genuine risk of the republican party being united under the leadership of men
like Sidney, Nevile, Marten, Wildman, and the author
of " Oceana." He therefore took pains to emphasise
the secular leanings of these men in order to prejudice the various sects, especially the Fifth Monarchy
men, against them.[1] He saw the weak point in Harrington's position. Harrington was not the atheist
that he was painted ; but he was well known to be the
friend of " religious Harry Nevile," who acknowledged
that he received as much inspiration from a passage in
Cicero as a passage in the Bible ; and he had himself
charged sectarian, Presbyterian, and Anglican alike
with hypocrisy. And, though in his writings he declared in emphatic terms his belief in the supreme
necessity of religion, he was not inspired with the
stern ideal of Puritanism and the burning desire to
introduce godliness at the point of the sword, which
characterised many of the actors in the Great Rebellion.

If Cromwell hoped to estrange the Fifth Monarchy men by pointing to Harrington's atheistical
tendencies, he hoped to estrange supporters of the
constitution of 1649 by a different argument. It was
not difficult to point out the novelty of the changes
advocated in " Oceana " ; for the institutions of
England were to be entirely re-shaped by Harrington's
schemes. Instead of a parliamentary government of
ancient lineage and historical sanction, a hotch-potch
of foreign constitutions was to be served up suddenly
in a country entirely unaccustomed to them. Where
indeed would the Long Parliament be in " Oceana " ?[2]

Both these arguments appealed very strongly to

---

[1] Burnet, " History of My Own Times," i. 120.
[2] Cf. Cromwell's Speech of Sept. 17, 1656 ; Carlyle, Speech V., Lomas ed.
ii. 547.

Cromwell himself. He could not understand how
people could argue, "Oh, if we could but exercise wisdom to get Civil Liberty—Religion would follow," and
he was voicing the sentiments of nearly all England
when he condemned Harrington for irreligion. As a
man of action he liked the doctrinaire elements of
"Oceana" little better than, as a Puritan, he liked its
secular tone. Almost an empiricist in politics, he
spoke in the bitterest terms of the "Constitution-
pedantries and parchments"[1] of men like Har-
ington, adding the Puritanical comment that their
"formalities," "notions," and "speeches" were not
satisfactory instruments "to defy all the opposition
that the Devil and man can make." Marchamont
Nedham pointed out in "Mercurius Politicus" that
"all forms of government are but temporary expedients to be taken upon trial, as necessity and right
reason of state enjoins, in order to the public safety ;
and that as 'tis a madness to contend for any form,
when the reason of it is gone, so 'tis neither dishonour
nor scandal, by following right reason, to shift through
every form, and after all other experiments made in
vain, when the ends of government cannot otherwise
be conserved, to revert upon the old bottom and
foundation."[2] Cromwell himself grew more and
more conservative as he felt his feet. In attempting
to secure the historical continuity which he desired,
and bridge over the biggest gaps that had been made he
was obliged to create an "other house" to replace the
House of Peers and accept the sceptre at the same time
as he refused the crown. Conservative minds looked
on contentedly at the gradual return to the conditions

[1] The phrase is Carlyle's.
[2] "Merc. Pol.," March 26-April 2, 1657, quoted in Firth, "Last Years of
the Protectorate," i. 160.

to which England had been acclimatised by many years of evolution. The protests of those who would begin over again were uttered in vain.

The series of letters from Utopia, which Nedham wrote in the " Mercurius Politicus " at the beginning of 1657, were the earliest of the many attempts to kill the Harringtonian doctrines with ridicule. Serious as well as satirical, Nedham adopted the conservative line of the Protector, whom his journal supported, and directed his shafts at the pedantry of every doctrinaire proposal that was brought forward. He deplored the " infectious itch of scribbling politicians " ; he described how the world had been " a maddening in disputes about Government, that is to say about Notions, Forms and Shadows " ; he depicted the landing of " a jolly crew of the inhabitants of the island of Oceana in company of the learned author himself " ; he proposed as a stringent remedy for this unfortunate tendency of the time the pensioning of a State Droll " as a most necessary officer to correct all that presume to Print or Dispute about Models of Government." [1]

Harrington was not put off by opposition or ridicule of this kind. Like all the writers of this tempestuous time he gloried in controversy, and deplored nothing which helped to advertise his opinions. He found an excuse to publish on January 3rd correspondence on the theories of " Oceana," which had taken place between himself and a clerical acquaintance of his sister's, Dr Ferne. He heard with delight the interest which he was creating at Oxford, where a gang of students boasted that they could produce forty examples in disproof of his doctrine of the balance.[2] And on August 14th he hailed the appearance of the

---

[1] " Mercurius Politicus," No. 352, E. 143.
[2] " The Prerogative of Popular Government," p. 380.

first serious pamphlet directed against " Oceana "
—the " Considerations on Mr Harrington's Commonwealth of Oceana," by Matthew Wren, the son of the
former Bishop of Ely.   On November 28th he issued
his " Prerogative of Popular Government " by way of
answer, seizing the opportunity of repeating his own
propositions at the same time as replying to his critic.
After this he took no rest.   He adopted the method of
compelling support by the sheer force of repetition, and
utilised every possible occasion to restate his position.

The year that followed did not present many opportunities.   The one that did occur was missed.   It
came in connection with the discussions on Cromwell's
" other house," which occupied the country during
the early part of 1658.   All the supporters of the
Protectorate recognised that some such check was
necessary to prevent the nation from giving up the
battle for Puritanism and calling back the King, but
they criticised the military character of its composition,
and objected that its members were " not a balance,
as the old Lords were, as to matter of estates." [1]   Here
was an opportunity which would have been no doubt
taken by Nevile.   But, though he had been a member
of the Long Parliament, he was not now in possession
of a seat.   And the reply, which must have exasperated
Harrington as much as it satisfied the Puritans, remained unanswered.   " These are the qualifications,
religion, piety, and faithfulness to the Commonwealth.
They are the best balance.   Those persons have it.
It is not estates will be the balance."   These debates,
which did nothing for Harrington beyond affording
him the satisfaction of seeing one of his theories hinted
at in Parliament, helped to revive other sections
of the republican party.   Those who desired to return

[1] Burton, " Diary," ii. 408

to the government of the Long Parliament were given new opportunities for advocating Single Chamber government; and in the confusion which ensued the Fifth Monarchy men were enabled to continue their plotting. But before the country had reached the point of instability at which political theory may run riot, Cromwell asserted his will and dissolved Parliament. With the army responsive to the magnetism of his personality and the discontent in the country lulled by the complete success of his foreign policy it seemed for a few weeks that the age of political experiment was over. But suddenly a light appeared in "Oceana." On September 3rd the man of action, who had done his utmost to keep the theorists in their proper place, died.

Harrington at once seized the occasion to repeat his views on republicanism in his pamphlet "Divers Models of Government." There was a renewed outbreak of faction. Although Richard Cromwell was accepted as Protector, a great part of the army was plainly disappointed that Fleetwood, Cromwell's son-in-law, had been passed over in favour of a civilian squire.

Many of the officers gathered round the Lieutenant-General at Wallingford House and proposed at least to separate the command of the army and the Protectorship. The republicans also began to meet at Sir Harry Vane's house in Charing Cross, to proclaim the illegitimacy of all forms of government but that of the Long Parliament, which had never been dissolved. In circumstances like these and with the memory of the behaviour of his father's last Parliament fresh in his mind Richard was compelled from want of money to summon a Parliament for January 27th, 1659. The reversion to the old distribution of seats, the inclusion of the Scotch and Irish Members who were

Cromwellian to a man, and the tricks of Richard's sheriffs could not prevent some critics and opponents from being elected.

Fifty republicans got in ; and Harrington's influence had been growing so steadily that ten of these were acknowledged followers of his. Harry Nevile was the best known of them, and he came into peculiar prominence during the course of the Parliament over his disputed election and his accusation for atheism and blasphemy. The next most active of the Harringtonians was a certain Captain Baynes, the member for Appleby. Having trafficked largely in delinquents' lands, purchasing an estate at Wimbledon, the Queen's property at Holdenby, and some royal forests in Lancashire, he was interested in a concrete sense in the doctrine of the balance of property ; and he appears himself to have been an official in charge of the sale of lands forfeited from the Crown or delinquents.[1] It is difficult to say to what extent the party was composed of men of this type ; but it is probable from the nature of the case that those who had bought land from the Commonwealth would be not only republicans but believers in the connection of power and property. When the debate turned, as it had turned a year before, on the important question of the " other house," the Harringtonians did not again miss their opportunity but asserted repeatedly and emphatically their theories.

They were not going to prejudice the new Protector or the House against them by attacking the government of a single person. " This man," said Nevile referring to Richard, " is, at least, actually, if not legally, settled the Chief Magistrate." " We that are for a Commonwealth, are for a single person, senate

<hr/>

[1] Cf. " Letters from Roundhead Officers," Bannatyne Club Publications, Introd. p. xiii and Letter 254.

and popular assembly." [1]   So they acquiesced in the
position of the Protector and confined their criticisms
to the power and constitution of the " other house."
Its existence they approved, because, unlike the other
republicans, they desired double-chamber government
as a part of their general system of checks and balances,
but they refused to accept anything but the system
which had been described in " Oceana."

Opinions in the house were various.   Enthusiasts
were there, who could say, " If all the world were paper
and sea ink they could not express liberty what it is." [2]
Cynics were there who could say, " I more dislike the
word Commonwealth than I did in the morning." [3]
Some were contented with a nominated Second
Chamber ; some added that it must include those of
the peers that had been loyal ; some proposed that
the peers should compose the nucleus of the Second
Chamber and that its numbers should be made up by
a mixture of nomination by the Protector and election
by the popular house, and nomination by the popular
house and election by the Protector ; some simply
asserted " that none shall sit in the Other House, but
such shall be approved by both Houses." [4]   All
realised the importance of the Second Chamber ; as
one member picturesquely put it, " the other house is
the balance ; it tells minutes between the two estates." [5]

Nevile made speech after speech in language remi-
niscent of Harrington.   One day he argued thus:
" The Commons till Henry VII never exercised a
negative voice.   All depended on the Lords.   In that
time it would have been hard to have found in this
house so many gentlemen of estates.   The gentry do
not now depend upon the peerage.   The balance is

---

[1] Burton, " Diary," iii. 132 and 133.   [2] *Ibid.* iii. 219.
[3] *Ibid.* iii. 344.   [4] *Ibid.* iii. 541.   [5] *Ibid.* iii. 339.

in the gentry. They have all the lands. Now Lords old or new must be supported by the people. There is the same reason why the Lords should not have a negative voice as that the King should not have a negative ; to keep up a sovereignty against nature. The people of England will not suffer a negative voice to be in those who have not a natural power over them." [1] Another day he urged : " We are upon an equal balance, which puts out Turkish government and peerage." [2] Another day he pointed out, in view of Harrington's proposals, that " the Other House may be such a House as is only preparatory to this, as, among popular assemblies in other commonwealths, there was an assembly to propound laws, and another to enact them, and a single person to put all in exe-cution." [3] Baynes followed Nevile's lead with equal vigour. In one place he ridiculed the idea of setting up " a house that has not so much interest as two Knights." [4] In another place he argued as follows : " All government is built on propriety, else the poor must rule it. . . . The people were too hard for the King in property ; and then in arms too hard for him. We must either lay the foundation in property or else it will not stand. Property generally is now with the people ; the government therefore must be there. If you make a single person he must be a servant and not a lord ; maior singulis, minor omnibus. If you can find a House of Lords to balance property, do it. Else let a senate be chosen by the election of the people on the same account. There must be a balance." [5] Elsewhere he continued thus : " The Lords represented at least in old time two-thirds of the rest, who having so great a propriety in the nation,

---

[1] Burton, " Diary," iii. 132 and 133. [2] *Ibid.* iii. 331.
[3] *Ibid.* iii. 321. [4] *Ibid.* iii. 31. [5] *Ibid.* iii 147.

it was all justice and reason they should have a co-ordination in the government. . . . It is my judgment to have two houses. And if we can find out such persons as have such proprieties as may balance this house by property in any considerable measure it is fit we should have them ; but if there be none such I would have another House, indeed, that there may be a propounding and an enacting power, but to be chosen either by the people or by some other way ; for there never was any Commonwealth but there was one body to propound laws and another to enact." [1]

Although certain members refused " to go back to past times or look forward to Oceana's Platonical Commonwealth ; things that are not and that never shall be," [2] yet a certain section of the house realised part of the truth of the Harringtonian position. Acknowledging Baynes' theory that " it is estates that make men Lords and esteemed in the country," [3] they proposed to find peers who could satisfy this principle. " It is objected," said one member, " that the Peers sat at first upon account of their ancient possessions, and their great proprieties and estates. And have they not so still, or if they have not, what have they that sit there ? I could name 5 or 6 of the ancient Peers that are not disabled from sittings that have estates and interests equivalent to buy out all that sit there now." [4] " There are," said another, " as great a number of peers who have not forfeited as were in the beginning of Queen Elizabeth's reign." [5] It was easy to argue that certain peers possessed more land than members of a popular assembly elected with but a small property qualification ; but the main point that the nation instead of a class was in possession

---

[1] Burton, " Diary," iii. 335. [2] Ibid. iii. 144.
[3] Ibid. iv. 31. [4] Ibid. iii. 542. [5] Ibid. iv. 27.

of the land could not be controverted. Never-theless the proposal to accept the facts and make the Second Chamber elective was not received with favour. Oliver's "other house," increased by a few of the old peers who had been faithful, was preferred.

The Parliament that turned a deaf ear to the Har-ringtonians was not destined to play a large part in history. By its support of Richard it widened the breach already existing between the civil government and the army. The Protector's attempt to counteract this by visiting Wallingford House and prohibiting future assemblies of officers was answered by threats from Fleetwood and Desborough, who on April 22nd succeeded in persuading Richard to dissolve Parlia-ment instead.

The confusion of the fortnight that ensued was great. The weakness and the royalist tendencies of Richard were becoming obvious. The army and the republicans were brought into closer sympathy by their common antagonism to the Protector. Fleetwood was almost master of the situation. But he had no serious intention of reverting to military rule. The plan that was preferred was the restoration of the Long Parliament. Haselrigge, Ludlow, Vane, and Scott, after having been suppressed by the two Protectors were at last to come to the fore.

The Harringtonians at once woke to renewed vigour. Harrington himself published on May 2nd a new pamphlet, entitled " Pour enclouer le Canon," in which he reasserted his theories of the proper con-stitution of a Commonwealth, and explained that the moment for their realisation had come. As the Long Parliament was to assemble, they could be introduced, as they should be, by the civil power. The people

would accept them, because their hankering after
monarchy meant no more than a desire to be governed
by laws and not by men.   On the same day certain
of Harrington's followers published a letter to Fleetwood, which had been composed on an earlier occasion.
They followed Harrington in pointing out the necessity
of having good *laws* ; good *men*, whether saints or
soldiers, are not a sufficient guarantee for liberty.
They declared that it was impossible to have both
liberty and a sovereign prince, and explained that
nations only consented to the existence of a monarch
when they saw " some great inequality and dispro-
portion between him and them in virtue, interest, or
power."   " An unequall interest in the lands may be
and is the common cause either of a voluntary or con-
strained subjection."   They then illustrated the
change in the ownership of property, which the last
century and a half had seen, and the consequent
alteration of the balance, " the greatest quantity
of the lands and with those the power being fallen
into the Commons' hands before the Warr, who
being then sensible, they neither depended upon
the King nor his peers for their bread, conceived
themselves obliged to serve none but God and therefore ought not to be commanded or have laws imposed upon them by the King or his Peers, judging
it the right of a people whose property rendered
them free and independent to choose their own laws
and magistrates being intended only for the preservation of their own properties and liberties."   They urged
Fleetwood to realise this and use the opportunity,
which his popularity gave him, to introduce a system
of " continual successive assemblies " consisting of
two chambers, one to debate and the other to resolve,
in preference to the tyranny of single chamber govern-

ment, which seemed the only other alternative to monarchy.[1]

After the lapse of a fortnight Harrington wrote a new pamphlet entitled, " A Discourse upon this Saying : The Spirit of the Nation is not yet to be trusted with Liberty ; lest it introduce Monarchy, or invade the Liberty of Conscience." Again he ridiculed the idea of a return to monarchy : " Let the more wary *Cavalier*," he wrote, " or the fiery *Presbyterian* march up when he may into the Van, he shall lead this Nation into a Commonwealth or into certain Perdition." Again he proposed the theories that he had proposed in " Oceana."

But the Long Parliament had in the meanwhile assembled. They were at once petitioned by the army to appoint a Select Senate co-ordinate in power with themselves. They, however, remained true to their principles of the supremacy of the House of Commons and did no more than form a Committee of Safety, consisting first of 7 and then of 11 members, afterwards increased to 31 (of which 21 were members of the house) and termed Council of State. The Harringtonians were not dismayed by the firmness of the Long Parliament. On June 14th, with Harrington's approbation they suggested that Parliament should be requested to form a committee for the purpose of discussing their propositions, and submitted a number of names for its composition. Their list included besides a few of their own number and certain of Harrington's relatives, persons with as varied opinions as those of Thurloe, Sir John Evelin, Prynne, Dr Owen, Sir Anthony Ashley Cooper, Sir George Booth, General Desborough,

[1] " The Armies' Duty," E. 787. The authors are given as H. M., H. N., I. L., I. W., I. I., S. M., Three of these stand without doubt for Henry Marten, Henry Nevile, and John Wildman. I. I. probably stands for John Jones.

and Praisegod Barebones.[1]   All the notice that was
taken of the suggestion was a scurrilous reply from
Prynne, suggesting that Harrington himself should be
included in the Committee and attend its meetings in
the true Grecian spirit with a rope round his neck.[2]

This rebuff had no effect on the party.   They continued still to repeat their proposals and defend their
position.[3]   An exhortation written in the true Miltonic
strain was issued.   " Where God Almighty in his
eternal Providence manifested to us in the present
time, hath thought fit to change and subvert old
foundations, and to lay new ones amongst us, let it
not be thought Novelty in those, who still to maintain
the building upright and firm, relinquish the old
rotten and obsolete foundations, and apply themselves
to the erecting of such agreeable superstructures on
those which are now laid amongst us, as shall be
most for the safety of the people, which is the Supreme
Law of all Nations." [4]   Following close upon this call
to activity Nevile presented to the house on July 6th
the Harringtonian manifesto, " The Humble Petition
of Divers Well-affected persons."   As the House
listened to the preamble, which asserted the doctrine
that authority rests on the consent of the people,
that single-chamber government is dangerous, even if
Parliament is subject to frequent elections, and that
the confusion of legislative and executive power is
deleterious to liberty, it might well have thought of
its own history.   Elected in 1640, although it was
for many years the sole chamber, it had enjoyed a
longer life than any previous Parliament in English

---

[1] " A Proposition in order to the Proposing of a Commonwealth."
[2] " An answer to a proposition," etc., E. 386.
[3] *Cf.* " A Commonwealth or Nothing," June 14th.   E. 986.
[4] " A Commonwealth of Commonwealths men Asserted and Vindicated,"
June 28th.   E. 988.

history ; during the first years of the Commonwealth, when the Council of State had been almost the same body as the House of Commons, it had possessed a more unbounded legislative and executive power than had ever been seen before in a free state ;[1] and now the forty-two of them that remained still claimed to be the representatives of the nation. " Their name and memorie stinkes," wrote Aubrey, " 'twas worse than tyranny."[2] The petition itself was a new digest of " Oceana." It consisted of a proposal for a Parliament consisting of two houses, one small for debating measures, the other large for voting on them, both of them subject each year to partial change by the scheme of rotation, an executive magistracy appointed by the legislative, and toleration for all Christians other than Roman Catholics. And insistence was now laid on an idea, which had been suggested without elaboration in " Oceana " and was now attracting considerable attention among republicans, including the Harringtonians. It was proposed to make it treason to suggest the restoration of monarchy or interference with religious liberty, and " Twelve persons of the most undoubted Fidelity and Integrity " were to be given the power to arrest any who made such proposals, to put them into custody, and to bring them to trial as traitors. In conclusion a further proposal, made as early as 1656 by Vane, and destined to play an important rôle in politics and to be adopted in the nineteenth century in many parts of the world, was added and expressed in the following words : " And if your Honours shall further judge it convenient, the Fundamental Orders

---

[1] Gardiner, " History of the Commonwealth and Protectorate," i. 8 and 9, points out that the average attendance in Parliament was 51, of whom 31 were also on the Council of State.

[2] " Brief Lives," i. 291.

of the Government may be consented unto or subscribed by the people themselves ; if their express Pact
shall be esteemed any additional security." The
petitioners were dismissed with all that they could have
expected, the formal thanks of the house. Harrington afterwards framed a fresh petition. But this
met with still less success, remaining unread in the
pockets of some two or three members.[1]

Pamphlets still continued to appear with great
frequency. On July 13th " Speculum Libertatis
Angliæ Re Restitutæ ; or the Looking-Glasse of
England's Libertie really Restored,"[2] an excellent
manifesto from someone in partial sympathy with
Harrington, was published. The writer proposed a
Fundamental Constitution for the three countries,
a new Magna Carta, which was to be read at stated
intervals and to be subscribed to originally by the
people. His religious settlement excluded Anglicans
as well as Roman Catholics from toleration, but otherwise resembled Harrington's. Parliaments were to
be triennial, appointing an executive and electing a
Council without legislative power, bearing the title,
" The Keepers of the Liberties of the Commonwealth
of England," to carry on the government in the intervals between Parliamentary sessions. Parliament
need have no more than one session—the fewer laws
and the fewer lawyers the better. The writer of
the pamphlet was far from suggesting the whole of
Harrington's scheme. But he accepted the additional
proposals of the petition of July 6th, and like Harrington made suggestions to avoid the tyranny of government by a single chamber and a Council of State as
exemplified by the Long Parliament.

Five days later a further tract entitled " Chaos,"[3]

[1] " Valerius and Publicola," p. 492.   [2] E. 989.   [3] E. 989.

poorer and more academic than the last, was published. It deserves notice as a variation or imitation of the theories of " Oceana." Its author began by explaining that he had borrowed but little from other countries, and in all cases reshaped what he had borrowed, to suit the different conditions. He then submitted his suggestions. His schemes for annual Parliaments elected indirectly, by ballot, and with a high property qualification for members, was rendered less workable than Harrington's by the omission of any system of nominating candidates. Members, who were to be paid and subject to periodical retirement, were divided into two classes, provincial and sub-provincial. The latter were to be elected at the beginning of each year for half a year only, and their votes were to have the value of one half a vote. A Council of State and a Committee for the Army and Navy were to be chosen by Parliament, partly from retiring and partly from newly elected members. Proposals were made for the proportional division of estates among all the children on the father's death. The institution of elaborate registers was suggested, so as to enable the government to adjust taxation fairly and know " who shall have responsible Estates fit to undergo any employment for the Republique." The reform of the poor law, education, and the guild system was foreshadowed ; and amongst other things public banks were recommended. The pamphlet was obviously written under the inspiration of Harrington, but it bears no comparison with " Oceana." It is aptly described by its title.

On July 28th Harrington repeated his objections to the régime of the Long Parliament and reasserted his belief in the hopelessness of the royalist position in his new tract, " A Discourse shewing that the Spirit

of Parliaments, with a Council in the Intervals, is not
to be trusted for a Settlement ;   lest it introduce
Monarchy and Persecution for Conscience."

By the summer of 1659 the Harringtonians had by
their importunity achieved notoriety.   Ludlow wrote of
the situation in the following terms : " At this time
the opinions of men were much divided concerning a
Form of Government to be established amongst us.
The great officers of the Army . . . were for a Select
Standing Senate to be joined to the Representation
of the People.   Others laboured to have the supreme
authority to consist of an Assembly chosen by the
People, and a Council of State to be chosen by that
Assembly to be vested with the executive power, and
accountable to that which should next succeed, at
which time the power of the said Council should
determine.   Some were desirous to have a Representative of the People constantly sitting, but changed by a
perpetual rotation.   Others proposed there might be
joined to the Popular Assembly a select number of men
in the nature of the Lacedæmonian Ephori, who should
have a negative in things, wherein the essentials of
the Government should be concerned, such as the exclusion of a Single Person, touching Liberty of Conscience, alteration of the Constitution, and other things
of the last importance to the State.   Some were of
opinion that it would be most conducive to public
happiness, if there might be two Councils chosen by
the people, the one to consist of about 300, and to have
the power only of debating and proposing laws ; the
other to be in number about 1000, and to have the
power finally to resolve and determine ; every year a
third part of each to go out and others to be chosen in
their places." [1]   Ludlow himself was inclined to favour

[1] Ludlow, " Memoirs," ii. 98-9.

Harrington's scheme in preference to either those of the senior or the junior officers, to which he alluded.

Harrington had repeated his theories twice more, in " Politicaster," a tract written in humorous vein against his critic Wren, and in " Aphorisms Political " ; and one of his supporters had urged the acceptance of nearly all his proposals except the decimal system in his " Model of a Democraticall Government," [1] when Dr Barwick wrote to Charles II. a somewhat similar description of the situation in England. " They at Westminster are as much perplexed as ever they were, being still full of fears and jealousies. Lambert [no longer Fleetwood] is suspected to drive a design for himself, from his unwonted civilities to a conquered enemy, and by pressing so often and earnestly for the soldiers' pay. The Army have as much reason to be jealous of the Parliament for continuing their levies of soldiers out of the congregated Churches under new commanders and notwithstanding the business is so far over as to put a stop to the militia ; and all of them are afraid of a storm from abroad. The engagement divides them very much. The Fifth Monarchy refuse to engage against a single person, lest they should exclude Christ, when he comes to reign ; and some that are not of their opinion are willing to abet their argument, under pretence of satisfying tender consciences. Others scruple at the words ' this Commonwealth,' till it be resolved what it shall be : which ordinarily takes up one day a week in debating. Some are for it as it is ; others with a co-ordinate senate ; others are taken with Harrington's new model. It were no irrational ground of hope that these divisions might be their ruin ; if we had not heretofore seen them cement upon the point of guilt, when it was not

[1] E. 986.

so great as now they have made it."[1] The strength
of Harrington's position lay in the consistency of his
views. People knew what he meant by a " Commonwealth." He never altered his definition of it as " a
Government consisting of the Senat proposing, the
People resolving, and the Magistracy executing." All
the pamphlets that he wrote were little more than
repetitions of his first book, " Oceana."

On September 28th the best of all the anonymous
writings of the Harringtonians appeared, " A Modest
plea for an Equal Commonwealth against Monarchy."[2]
The writer began like all the constitution-makers by
pointing out the opportuneness of the moment for the
political theorist. " God hath put the Nation like
wax into your hands, that you may mould and cast
it into what Form your honours please." He warned
the wavering country against any form of monarchy,
elective and hereditary alike, excepting possibly that
type where the monarch is nothing but a Doge or figure-
head. He pointed out that the royal " we " is in
itself an argument against the rule of a single person.
He attacked the hereditary principle in the House of
Peers, and proposed with Harrington an elective
Second Chamber. " Since no choice can be more
perilous than the casual lot of nature, I had rather
stand to any election than mere chance ; by reason we
have oftener known fools the sons of wise men by
nature, than of the people's choice or adoption." He
criticised the system of land tenure, by which the
eldest son received the whole of his father's landed
property, and the younger sons, now excluded by sec-
tarianism from the Church, overcrowded the detested
legal profession. He argued against giving power to
corporations, because " all Trades have been over-

---

[1] Carte, " Original Letters," ii. 203. [2] E. 999.

stocked," and trading people are generally " sheepish and tame citizens." He upheld compulsory military training. He went through Harrington's proposals for an agrarian, a scheme of double election, and rotation. And though he did not believe in a too great extension of education, he outlined a scheme for the reform of the universities. The only point in which he refused to follow his leader was the religious settlement. He accepted the connection of civil and religious liberty, which Harrington had asserted, but instead of a secular magistracy sharply distinguished from a paid clergy he desired the rule of godly persons, the dominion of the saints, people described by Harrington as " those that would have the Government be somewhat between Earth and Heaven." [1]

By the beginning of the autumn the situation had somewhat changed. Royalist activity was greater than ever, and Sir George Booth had attempted a rising in Cheshire, which had been put down by Lambert. The army was growing more insolent, claiming permanent appointments not only for Fleetwood and Desborough, but for Monk and Lambert, who was rumoured to be aiming at the Protectorship. The Long Parliament became disunited. Vane deserted them. On October 13th Lambert appeared at Westminster with troops, and by threats and intimidation persuaded the unfortunate house to dismiss and leave the duty of summoning another to the Council of Officers. The old Council of State was allowed to continue its duties, and the Council of Officers still met. For a fortnight the double rule of a civil and military aristocracy, which Milton hoped to make permanent [2] and Harrington detested, was

---

[1] " The Prerogative of Popular Government," p. 367.
[2] *Cf.* Masson, "Life of Milton," v. 621.

given a trial. On October 26th the Council of State
was replaced by the Committee of Safety—a body of
twenty-three persons including Lambert, Fleetwood,
Desborough, Vane, and Ludlow.[1]

The confusion and uncertainty of the months that
followed have never been equalled. Proposals for a
new constitution now poured forth more freely than
they had ever done. People felt the inevitability of
the restoration of the monarchy, and tried in vain either
to struggle or shut their eyes against it. The more
ardent their republicanism, the more unwilling they
were to play into the hands of their opponents by accepting the restoration of the Rump, the Long Parliament, or Richard's late Parliament. Army leaders
and republicans alike agreed that some body of the
nature of the Spartan Ephorate must be created to
guard whatever constitution was decided on, and to
prevent the restoration of monarchy. Some proposed to give this body the power of summoning
Parliament and initiating all legislation, as well as an
absolute veto. Some proposed that it should consist
of 3, some of 21, some of 40, and some of the
magic number of which the Sanhedrim had been
composed—70. Some would call it a Senate, some an
Inquisitory, some the " Conservators of the principles
of the Commonwealth." The proposal that bore the
strongest marks of Harrington's influence was one that
was suggested in the Committee of Safety but never
published. According to this the government of the
country was to be entrusted to two councils, consisting
of 50 and 200 members, respectively, the former
elected by the people from 400 names submitted to
them by the 50. Each year 10 members were to
retire from the smaller council and be replaced out of

---

[1] Masson, v. 454.

the larger. But this was too fanciful to have any chance of acceptance. The majority of the leading politicians still adhered to the old system of Single Chamber Government with a Council of State. The only novelty that was adopted was the " Conservators of Liberty " ; and this was not due to Harrington or even to Vane but to the importunity of Ludlow. But the house of representatives, Council of State, and Conservators of Liberty never undertook the government of the country. Few could have anticipated a permanent settlement if they had. With one of those sudden movements which are only found in the political crises of great cities, the Rump was called back to office on December 26th, to retire for the last time on February 21st, 1660, in response to unparalleled popular ridicule.[1]

The period of instability and anarchy which lasted from Lambert's *coup d'état* of October 13th to Monk's final expulsion of the Rump was the golden age for the Harringtonians and all other doctrinaire politicians. Harrington continued to pour forth his stream of pamphlets. On October 18th he answered his antagonist, John Rogers, who had delivered an attack on him in his " Διαπολιτεία," [2] from the standpoint of the Puritan oligarch. The reply, which was entitled, " A Parallel of the Spirit of the People with the Spirit of Mr Rogers," is worthless and uninteresting. Harrington realised this, and with that naïveté and charm, which we know from other sources he possessed, added a footnote which serves as an ample compensation. " Reader, I entreat your pardon, I Know well enough that this is below me ; but something is to be yielded to the Times ; and it hath been

[1] Guizot, " Richard Cromwell," i. 185, 474 ; ii. 286, 290 ; Masson, " Life of Milton," v. 511 ; Carte, " Original Letters," ii. 248, etc. [2] E. 995.

an Employment of two or three Hours in a rainy Day." [1]
One can forgive dulness for that. On November 7th,
" Valerius and Publicola " appeared. It was written
in the form of a dialogue, being an attempt to set forth
in the simplest and most popular manner possible
Harrington's idea of republicanism and double-chamber
government. On January 9th, 1660, a fresh epitome
of " Oceana " was published in a pamphlet entitled
" The Rota." On February 8th, Harrington suggested the actual procedure advisable for the introduction of his proposals in " The Ways and Means
whereby an Equal and Lasting Commonwealth may
be suddenly introduced," etc. And on the day before
Monk dismissed the Rump, " The Art of Lawgiving,"
and the " Word Concerning the House of Peers "
appeared.

Harrington's activity helped to produce the increasing notoriety to which it was itself due. As
early as February 1659, the remnant of the Levellers
declared themselves in favour of his proposals.[2]
Monk's remark that " Monarchy cannot possibly be
admitted for the future in these nations, because its
support is taken away," was construed as an acceptance of Harrington's theory of the balance.[3] Ludlow,
in close sympathy with him on the question of the
Ephorate, was for a time converted to the teachings
of " Oceana." [4] Vane wrote to Harrington to express
his admiration of his work.[5] His " cabal," as his
following was sometimes called, was acknowledged to

---

[1] " Works," p. 618.

[2] *Cf.* Harl. Misc. iv. 544. " The Leveller," a manifesto published on
February 16th, 1659.

[3] " Animadversions on the letter to the Gentry of Devon," etc., E 1015.

[4] " Memoirs," ii. 99.

[5] " A Needful Corrective or Ballance in Popular Government expressed in
a letter to James Harrington, Esquire." Bodleian Library. The sentence
with which the Puritan prefaces his admiration deserves quotation. " Where

be second in importance on the republican side to
Haselrigge's party.[1]

This notoriety was voiced in the fugitive literature
of the time ; and Harrington's fame was enhanced by
the names with which he was coupled.

> " Scot, Nevil and Vane
> With the rest of that train
> Are into Oceana fled ;
> Sir Arthur the brave,
> That's as arrant a knave
> Has Harrington's Rota in's head." [2]

wrote a song writer in March 1660. " And now
John," wrote a royalist pamphleteer addressing Milton,
as he stands on the scaffold, " *you* must stand close and
draw in your elbows that Needham, the Commonwealth didapper, may have room to stand beside you.
. . . He was one of the spokes of Harrington's Rota,
till he was turned out for cracking. As for Harrington he's but a demy-semy in the Rump's musick and
should be good at the cymbal, for he is all for wheeling
instruments." [3] No other public character was more
ridiculed. In the numerous lampoons of the time
Harrington and his notorious coffee-club are alluded
to with unfailing regularity. Sandwiched between
indecent remarks or bits of satire, passages like the
following occur—in " Bibliotheca Militum " or an
imaginary soldier's library, " Heyte Tyte, or to-morrow
morning I found an Horse-shoe ; being an excellent
discourse concerning Government, with some sober
and practical expedients, modestly propos'd and

(as you all along most deservedly have regard unto) the Foundations of
Government shall be laid so firm and deep as in the Word of God, bottomed
upon that Corner-Stone the Lord Jesus, there is a Heavenly Ballance to be
met with, which keeps all even."

[1] Carte, " Original Letters," ii. 225.
[2] " Political Ballads of the Commonwealth," iii. 215.
[3] " Character of the Rump," E 1017.

written by James Harrington," also, " A new gag for
an old Goose or a reply to Mr James Harrington's
Oceana by Mr Wrenn " [1]—in " Bibliotheca Fanatica "
or the imaginary fanatic's library, " The Rump's
Seminary, or the best way to find out the ablest Utopian
Commonwealths men, by the Coffee Club at Westminster " [2]—in Alazonomastix Philalethes' " Free
Parliament Queries," " Whether Hanging or Drown-
ing be the best waies of Transportation of our late
Republicans to the Commonwealths of Utopia or
Oceana " [3]—in " A new map of England or 46
queries," " Whether Dr Owen's infant Commonwealth
was not an Anabaptist, since he nor Mr Harrington
could give it a name." " Whether Mr Harrington is
studying Monarchy or an Aristocracy now, since his
Democraticall Government took no effect." " Whether
he did not take great pains to no purpose " [4]—in the
" Decrees and Orders of the Committee of Safety of
the Commonwealth of Oceana," I. " That the
Politick Casuists of the Coffee Club in Bow Street
appoint some of their number to instruct the Committee of Safety at Whitehall how they shall finde an
Invention to escape Tyburne, if ever the Law be
restored " ; II. " That Harrington's Aphorisms and
other Political slips be recommended to the English
Plantation in Jamaica, to see how they will agree with
that Apocryphal Purchase " ; III. " That a Levite
and an Elder be sent to Survey the Government of
the Moon and that Warreston Johnston and Parson
Peters be the Men, as a couple of Learned Rabbies in
the Lunaticks." [5] The burlesque proposal to ship
Harrington to Jamaica was a common one.[6] Little
did Samuel Butler, when he proposed " That Mr

[1] E 986.   [2] E 1956.   [3] E 1001.   [4] E 1010.
[5] Cf. " Democritus turned Statesman," E 1985.   [6] " 38 Queries," E 988.

Harrington be forthwith despatched to Jamaica, that
famous island, and form his commonwealth there," [1]
know that Harrington's ideas were destined to go a
little further, find acceptation on the mainland of
America, and be embodied in the constitution of the
United States.

As early as 1656 Harrington had conducted with
more or less regularity a campaign in support of his
propaganda among the London coffee-houses. In
November 1659, he formed his famous Rota Club of
which Aubrey, himself a member, has left a short description. "He had every night a meeting at the
(then) Turke's head, in the New Pallace-yard, where
they take water, the next house to the staires, at one
Miles's, where was made purposely a large ovall-table
⌒, with a passage in the middle for Miles
to deliver his coffee. About it sate his disciples and
the virtuosi. The discourses in this kind were the
most ingenoise, and smart that ever I heard, or expect
to heare, and bandied with great eagernesse ; the arguments in the Parliament-house were but flatt to it.
Here we had (very formally) a balloting-box, and
balloted how things should be carried by way of ten-
tamens. The room was every evening full as it could
be cramm'd." [2] The idea of forming the club was
perhaps suggested by the academies, which Harrington had seen in various towns in Italy. In London
there had been nothing of the sort before. The Royal
Society, whose meetings had now begun, was purely
scientific. The republican meetings in Vane's house
in Charing Cross had been of a private but practical
nature. The Calves Head Club, which was said to have

---

[1] " Acts and Monuments of our Late Parliament," Harl. Misc. v. 423.
[2] Aubrey, " Brief Lives," ii. 289-90.

been formed " by Milton and some other creatures of
the Commonwealth in opposition to Bishop Juxon,
Dr Sanderson, Dr Hammond and other divines of the
Church of England, who met privately every 30th of
January," the anniversary of Charles I.'s martyrdom,
was either a fiction or a republican club of later date.
The Rota Club was a novelty, and for that reason
popular. It was open to all. One night Bohemians
like Pepys or Aubrey would drop in ; another night
aristocrats like Sir John Penruddock or the Earl of
Tyrconnel. Every meeting was packed with officers
and soldiers. Some nights debates would be held
smoothly enough ; other nights a gang of drunk men
would burst into the house and create a scuffle,
for the tactful Harrington to quell. In the coffee-
drinking atmosphere of the modern debating society
people would see Venice in the bright balloting urns
and balls, Rome in the shape of the table. They
would indulge in politics without the dust of the
political arena. Practical politics were barred. Harrington posed as a private gentleman interested in state-
craft and particularly ready to point to the lessons of
Roman history. He had no desire to plot or form
conspiracies. All he wanted was to get his theories
of government known and understood. If this was
done, he felt confident that out of the turmoil and the
anarchy some English Napoleon would arise and establish Oceana in England.

The name of the club was taken from the revolving
contrivance used for receiving votes at papal elections ;
so that there was a suggestion of the ballot as well as
rotation in its very title. The club had its minutes,
its membership and its chairman. The minutes were
kept by Harrington. The chair was taken by Milton's
friend, Cyriac Skinner, or by Sir William Poulteney.

Members were a varied lot, some having interests primarily academic, some interests primarily political. Comparatively well known people like Nevile, Wildman, Venner, Aubrey, Robert Wood, Sir Edward Coke's grandson, Maximilian Petty, and Petty the economist must be put besides unknown names like those of Malett, Ford, Gold, Morley, Collins, and Morgan.

Francis Cradoc was a merchant, who afterwards became provost-marshal of Barbados, where he instituted banks founded on security of land for the encouragement of trade[1]; Bagshaw was a member of Christchurch, Oxford; Marriet was a Warwickshire squire. Philip Carteret was a gentleman from the Channel Isles belonging to a family that was to be prominent in the colonial enterprise of the Restoration period and provide the name for the plantation of New Jersey. Croon or Croom was a physician, Sir John Hoskyns a future President of the Royal Society, and Arderne a gentleman who either was at the time or soon became a divine, and was therefore somewhat ashamed of his connection with the club. It is not without interest to know the names of the principal Rota-men, but it is far more important to remember the number of casual spectators, who dropped in nightly to hear the speeches and watch the procedure.[2]

The procedure may be inferred from two or three accounts of the club, which have come down to us. The rules are preserved in Harrington's pamphlet, the " Rota."

" At the Rota. Decem. 20. 1659.

[1] Cal. State Papers, Col. Series, 1661-8, nos. 194 and 260.
[2] Aubrey, " Brief Lives," i. 288-93 and ii. 148 ; Wood, " Athenæ Oxonienses," iii. 115 ff. ; " The Rota," Collection of Loyal Songs, ii. 214.

" Resolved, that the Proposer be desired, and is hereby desired to bring in a Model of a Free State, or equal Commonwealth, at large, to be farther debated by this Society, and that in Order thereunto it be first Printed.

" Resolved, that the Model being proposed in Print, shall be first read, and then debated by Clauses.

" Resolved, that a Clause being read over Night, the Debate thereupon begin not at the sooner till the next Evening.

" Resolved, that such as will debate, be desired to bring in their Queries upon, or Objections against the Clause in Debate, if they think fit in writing.

" Resolved, that Debate being sufficiently had upon a Clause, the Question be put by the Balloting-box, not any way to determine of, or meddle with the Government of these Nations, but to discover the Judgment of this Society, upon the form of Popular Government, in Abstract, or *Secundum Artem.*" [1]

These rules illustrate in a striking form the intentions of the club and the orderly way in which business was carried out.

It appears from a contemporary song called " The Rota " that the ballot was not used, until it had first been found out by acclamation, whether there was any doubt concerning the views of the house.

> " If unresolved by I or Not
> It must be put to the Ballot,
> T'is Mr Harrington's own Plot." [2]

This is borne out by Pepys' account of one of his visits to the club. " I went," he writes on January 17th,

---

[1] " Works," p. 621.   [2] " Collection of Loyal Songs," ii. 214.

1660, " to the Coffee Club [Miles'] and heard very good discourse ; it was in answer to Mr Harrington's answer, who said that the state of the Roman Government was not a settled government, and so it was no wonder that the balance of prosperity [1] was in one hand, and the command in another, it being therefore always in a posture of war ; but it was carried by ballot that it was a steady government, though it is true by the voices it had been carried before that it was an unsteady government ; so to-morrow it is to be proved by the opponents that the balance lay in one hand and the government in another."   The academic nature of the Society, which is here seen, is further illustrated by Butler's satirical " Speech made at the Rota," [2] and by the somewhat futile song which has been already quoted, with the stanza,

> First Harrington doth hawk and hum
> And tells a story of old Rome
> Which from his own store never come."

A further account of an evening at the club may be found in " The Censure of the Rota upon Mr Milton's Book, entitled ' The Ready and Easy Way to establish a free Commonwealth,' " etc. [3]

The pamphlet purported to be written by Harrington and was signed with the initials J. H.   But it is not hard to see that it is a mere royalist squib. However, it is of none the less historical value, because, burlesque as it is, it bears out our other accounts. The imprint on the title-page shows the secretary being commanded to draw up a detailed minute of the proceedings.   " Die Lunæ, 26° Martii 1660.   Ordered by the Rota, that Mr Harrington be desired to draw up a

---

[1] Pepys has mistaken the phrase " Balance of Property."
[2] " Genuine Remains," i. 317.
[3] Harl. Misc. iv. 188 and E 1019 ; cf. Masson, " Life of Milton," v. 659.

Narrative of this Day's Prooceeding upon Mr Milton's Book, called, ' The Ready and Easy Way,' etc. And to cause the same to be forthwith printed and published, and a Copy thereof to be sent to Mr Milton. Trundle Wheeler, Clerk to the Rota." "Printed at London by Paul Giddy, Printer to the Rota, at the sign of the Windmill in Turn-again Lane, 1660." There is no reason to suppose that this is not a correct account of the procedure at the Rota ; but the date March 26th, the name of the clerk, the printer, the sign, and the lane, in which the printing works are supposed to be, show without doubt the nature of the publication. The evening of which a picture is given was devoted to a criticism of Milton's political philosophy as illustrated by his latest book. Generally opinion at the Rota was pretty evenly divided, because Harrington always encouraged the attendance of opponents and men of every kind of view ; but on this occasion hardly anyone could be found to defend Milton. After several speeches of somewhat cheap invective, a gentleman that had been some years beyond seas rose and delivered a speech of a more academic nature. But in the course of his remarks a diversion took place " He was interrupted by a gentleman that came in, and told us, that Sir Arthur Hazlerig, the Brutus of our republick, was in danger to be torn to pieces, like a Shrove-tuesday bawd, by the boys in Westminster Hall ; and if he had not shown himself as able a footman as he that cudgelled him, he had gone the way of Dr Lamb infallibly. This set all the company alaughing ; and made the traveller forget what he was going to say." So somebody else got up and started an attack on Milton's prejudice against royalty, blaming him for taking his philosophy out of the writing of Greek demagogues, and reminding him of a certain biblical phrase, "The Kingdom of Heaven." His successor attempted wit. They then balloted on Milton's views of monarchy. One speech of a more sensible nature followed, and the company got tired. So a worthy knight got up and protested against continuing a subject, which seemed never likely to end, summed up, used invective, pointed out the absurdity of believing that all Kings are bad and all commonwealths good, and made a peroration in praise of Charles II. But Harrington himself was asked to make a speech, before the club dismissed. He blamed Milton for making no reference to the Agrarian and for refusing to accept the principle of rotation, he discoursed in brief on Rome and Venice, he compared the nation to a top, which does not stand unless it spins, and he recommended his balloting balls as good pills for a body that is diseased. And so the evening ended.

Allowance must be made for the royalist authorship of the pamphlet. It is doubtful indeed whether the club would have ever attacked a man who was in many ways in sympathy with them. Otherwise, however, it may serve as a vivid picture of an evening at the club, written by someone who had paid it a visit as a spectator. The report of Harrington's own speech may be compared with a passage in Aubrey illustrating his fondness for homely similes. " He was wont to find fault with the constitution of our government, that 'twas *by jumps*, and told the story of a cavaliero he sawe at the Carnival in Italie, who rode on an excellent managed horse that with a touch of his toe would jump quite round. One side of his habit was Spanish, the other French ; which sudden alteration of the same person pleasantly surprized the spec- tators." " Just so," said he, " 'tis with us. When no Parliament, then absolute monarchie ; when a Parliament, then it runnes to a Commonwealth." [1] But by March 26th, the Rota was no longer in existence. On February 20th or 21st, " upon the unexpected turne upon General Monke's comeing in, all these aierie modells vanished." [2] Pepys went on what was perhaps the last night of its existence and " heard Mr Harrington and my Lord of Dorset and another Lord, talking of getting another place at the Cockpit, and they did believe it would come to something." But " the club," he adds, " broke up very poorly, and I do not think they will meet any more." We do not know if they ever did ; we draw the curtain on the picture of Harrington, still hopeful, discussing with two members of the English aristocracy, which he so much admired, the prospect of future meetings.

Dr Johnson wrote of Milton—" Even in the year of the restoration he bated no jot of heart or hope but was fantastical enough to think that the nation, agitated as it was, might be settled by a pamphlet." Guizot wrote of Vane—" It is a peculiarity of subtle and chimerical minds to believe that success is always possible." What Dr Johnson wrote of Milton and Guizot of Vane might equally well be applied to Harrington. He was not disheartened by the acceptance of forms of government that differed from his own, and he had no serious fears of the restoration of the old monarchical system. He thought it impossible under existing economic conditions. Aubrey recounts the following prophetic remark of Harrington in reference to the return of Charles II. and the Cavalier Parliament—a remark which appears in various forms in his writings. " Let him come in and call a Parliament of the greatest Cavaliers in England,

---

[1] Aubrey, " Brief Lives," i. 291.   [2] *Ibid.*

so they be men of estates, and let them sitt but 7 yeares, and they will all turn Common-wealthe's men." The half-truth in this conjecture is obvious. Harrington's optimism, however, waned before long ; and though republicans like Pierpoint and St John were still active, Harrington had by the middle of March given up all hope.[1]

His theories, however, still attracted some attention, when their author had retired. Either at the beginning of March or the end of February Milton, who was now champion of the republican party, published his " Ready and Easy Way to establish a Free Commonwealth," to which reference has already been made. He still adhered to his belief in the necessity of permanence in government. " The Ship of the Commonwealth is always under sail ; they sit at the stern ; and if they steer well, what need is there to change them ; it being rather dangerous ? " He therefore proposed the election of a Grand Council with life membership, electing a smaller Council of State. He did not believe in the advisability of alternation or rotation in government. He thought it impaired the dignity of office, made the acquisition of experience impossible, and meant the widespread divulgence of state secrets. For the further security of liberty he suggested a form of decentralised government, which almost amounted to federalism. But if people were sceptical or dissatisfied, rather than fall back on the ordinary proposals for annual, biennial, or triennial parliaments, he expressed his readiness to accept a modification of Harrington's ideas, by which a portion of the Grand Council would retire every second or third year. This, however, was his δεύτερος πλούς.

---

[1] Clarendon, " State Papers," iii. 701.

The squib written against this pamphlet to which
reference has already been made appeared at the end
of March.[1] Milton read it, and, whether he believed
Harrington had written it or not, published some
time in April a second edition of his tract, in which
he made alterations and additions by way of
answering the squib. He made the general criticism
of Harrington's theories as " intricacies," " exotic
models," " ideas that would effect nothing, but with
a number of new injunctions to manacle the native
liberty of mankind."

In particular he objected to the idle and unwieldy
popular assembly of Harrington's scheme with its
frivolous paraphernalia. He realised as much as
Harrington the need of well-qualifying and refining
elections so as not to " commit all to the noise and
shouting of a rude multitude." But he mistrusted
the ballot. So he proposed a system of indirect
election far more stringent than Harrington's. He
would permit none but those " who are rightly qualified
to nominate as many as they will ; and out of that
number others of a better breeding to choose a less
number more judiciously ; till after a third or fourth
sifting and refining of exactest choice, they only be
left chosen, who are the due number, and seem by most
voices the worthiest." He still believed that life
membership was safe as long as the army of the godly
party remained in existence ; and he still hoped his
federal system would help to prevent tyranny in the
Grand Council and secure liberty for the people. The
fact that Milton gave as much prominence and as
much sympathy to Harrington's proposals as he did,
helps to show that they did not pass with their author
into oblivion.

[1] See above, p. 105.

On April 25th, the Convention Parliament assembled, and the republicans gave up their last hope.
The restoration of monarchy was certain ; the Commonwealth was dead.   Anyone who read the reprint
of Vane's " Healing Question " must have paused when
he came to this sentence : " In this tract of time,
there hath been (as we may say) a great silence in
heaven."   It was what every royalist was thinking of
the last twelve years.   One of them writing the day
after the meeting of the Convention Parliament used
words, which not only illustrate the dominant feeling
of the time but serve to sum up the success and the
failure of " Oceana."   The author, after accepting
Harrington's main proposition that dominion follows
landed property, and arguing that for this very
reason a " free state " or democracy is impossible
for a country possessing the caste of " gentlemen,"
which England possesses, continued as follows : " But
t'will be said, as Plato fancied his Community, and
Sir Thomas More his Utopia, so may we a Rotation,
thereby to gather up a new model of a Commonwealth out of the scattered gentry, in the nature of a
House of Commons.   Truly my friends, if you will try
new experiments, I wish you had other subjects to
practice upon, than the Estates and Lives, nay, the
very souls of Christians.   We have run the loss of those
and the hazard of these too long upon the hopes of a
Chimæra in the brains of some.   The word Liberty has
deluded us into patience, and patience since 48 has
brought forth less payments, but more servitude."
Then after condemning the Commonwealth of Oceana,
one of the chief principles of which he had accepted,
he concluded on the monarchical note which ushered
in Charles II.   " The English gentry have spirits pure,
naturally just, and generous like fire aspiring as a

pyramid, from low to high, and it will never rest, till it contracts itself into a Unity at top : so God is one, or he were not God, nor could he rule the world." [1]

[1] " A Discourse for a King and Parliament," W. C. Gg. 310. British Museum Catalogue.

CHAPTER V

HARRINGTON not unnaturally aroused a great deal of criticism of an academic nature. In the four years which have just been described Matthew Wren, the son of the Bishop of Ely, Henry Stubbe of Christ Church, Oxford, John Rogers, the enthusiastic supporter of the Long Parliament, Captain Bray, the sectarian soldier, and Richard Baxter, the Presbyterian preacher all took up their cudgels against him. Harrington himself started controversies with Dr Ferne, Dr Heylyn, Dr Seaman, and Dr Hammond. Hobbes, in spite of all Harrington's challenges (Aubrey says that " Oceana " was written against him[1]), remained silent.

Much of what was written on both sides is very uninteresting. Discussions on the method of ordination in the early Christian Church were followed by disputes about the origin, composition, and functions of the Sanhedrim. The exact powers of the tribunes and ephors in checking arbitrary action were mooted. The constitution of Sparta formed a subject for controversy. Wren showed very capably that neither Aristotle nor Thucydides had the slightest conception of the balance of property, and made a happy quotation from Anacharsis with reference to Harrington's two chambers, " That wise men propounded Matters and Fools decided them." Stubbe wrote at length of the " historical defects of Oceana." Harrington had a

---

[1] " Brief Lives," i. 366.

fairly extensive knowledge of ancient history, but he
sometimes made mistakes. All the controversies that
arose over them are almost valueless now. For one
who professed to use the historical method in political
science inaccuracy was not desirable. But it makes
no difference, to Harrington's practical conclusions,
if the parallels illustrating them could be in certain cases proved to be false parallels ; the results
remained exactly the same.

The novelty and Utopian character of Harrington's
proposals came in for not unexpected criticism.
Oceana was called " an aery, empty and imaginary
Utopia, the Phanatiques' Land of Forgetfulness." [1]
Attacks were levelled at " Rotations and Fantastical
Elections, which are no way grounded on the people's
choyce and besides, lay no foundation of Settlement,
as being unpracticable." [2] The general craze for
hankering after new models of government was condemned. " Models of new government heal not,"
said Dr Gauden from the pulpit, " Government must
fit the genius of a people." [3] Imitations of foreign
institutions were decried on all hands, and the tendency
to turn to Sparta, Athens, Venice, or the Netherlands
as models for the English constitution was widely
deprecated.[4] The natural growth of the monarchical
institutions of England was the common argument
against republicanism.[5] Baxter, in adding his voice to
the protests of others, criticised the prevailing tendency from the religious as well as the political point
of view, employing language which would seem amazing
if used in any other age. As a Puritan he objected to

[1] " Select City Queries," E 1019.
[2] " The Interest of England stated," E 125.
[3] " Κάκουργοι sive Medicastri ; slight healers of public hurts," E 1019
[4] Cf. " Vox vere Anglorum or England's loud cry for their King," E 125.
[5] " Shield against the Parthian dart," E 988.

Oceana, " in that it is such a government as heathens have been our examples in, and in which he [Harrington] thinks they have excelled in," and also because it is based on the practice of Venice, " where Popery ruleth and whoredom abounds." [1] But Harrington was blamed not only for the novelty of his ideas but also for his want of originality. He was reminded that many people had for a long time realised the connection of power and property. That is the worst of it. When something new is discovered, it is generally proved to be either old or faddy and pedantic.

His idealism and fondness for " exotic models " was criticised. So was his audacity in interfering at all in politics. The words of Stubbe may stand for many others. " I beseech you Sir," he wrote, " are not we writers of Politiques a somewhat ridiculous sort of People ? Is it not a fine piece of folly for private men sitting in their Cabinets to rack their brains about models of Government ? " [2] Burnet, in his account of the last days of the Commonwealth, explained how that " to see a few persons take upon them to form a scheme of government . . . made many conclude it was necessary to call home the King, that so matters might again fall into their old channel." [3] But what annoyed Harrington very much more, was the opinion given by Dr Ferne that private gentlemen ought not to meddle in religion either.[4] Harrington disagreed strongly with the view that politics was a profession. The exclusion of the layman from religious controversy seemed to him the grossest form of priestcraft.

Many of the criticisms, which were passed on the democratic ideal, have already been alluded to in the

[1] Baxter, " Holy Commonwealth," pp. 225-26.
[2] Preface to " Considerations on Mr Harrington's Commonwealth of Oceana," etc.   [3] " History of My Own Time," i. 151.
[4] " Pian Piano," p. 559.

course of this essay.   Certain objections are common
to all ages.   It will always be urged that the people
in a national community have no more rights of sovereignty than the members of a school or of any for-
tuitous aggregation of men ; that the majority is
frequently worse than the minority, because government is an " aptitude " for which the common man
is not fitted ; that the people as a whole are neither
wise, educated, leisured, moral, united, suited for
secret or speedy work, stable, or merciful.   This was
what Baxter urged.[1]   But such arguments were intended to be supplementary to the more cogent arguments from Scripture, which dominated the whole
controversy between democracy and the divine rights
of kings.   The real objection was one that is typical
of the age with which we are dealing.   Democracy
is the worst form of government, because it differs
most from the government of God and His angels,
and " comes nearest to the utter confounding of
governors and governed : the ranks that God separated
by His institutions." [2]   Criticisms like Baxter's were
too vague to be valuable.   They were also unfair.
Harrington confined direct popular interference to
three points—the right of electing representatives,
the right of petitioning parliament, the right of sub-
scribing consent to the constitution, under which the
country is to be governed.   Baxter himself, when he
descended to details, was ready to grant " that the
People's Consent is ordinarily necessary to the Constitution of the Government, and that their Freedom
is taken from them, when this is denied them." [3]
But, speaking for the Presbyterian party as a whole,
he was bound to add " we believe that notorious
wickedness and divers particular crimes may forfeit

[1] " Holy Commonwealth," p. 67, etc.   [2] *Ibid.* p. 89.   [3] *Ibid.*, Preface.

this freedom as to particular persons." Stubbe went further than Baxter and condemned Harrington unmercifully for making the consent of the people the origin of government. Looking back from the impartial point of view of the historian we may pass over Stubbe's remark, and rather compliment Harrington for his moderation in using this doctrine. He never touched the Social Contract. He stuck to facts.

More subtle and more interesting were the criticisms which were levelled at the limited form of indirect democracy which Harrington actually advocated. Curious objections were brought against the representative system as a whole. Baxter pointed out the difficulty of reconciling it with the doctrines of direct democracy, because the power, which the people have, of " choosing the persons that they have " is different from " the power of governing." He objected further to the tyranny of the majority, based on the democratic principle that " might is right " and inevitably bound up in the parliamentary system.[1] Sir Robert Filmer condemned the system on the ground that each representative ought to represent the entire nation and not merely a locality.[2] Wren brought a not dissimilar criticism. " The Concernments of the severall parts of this Nation," he wrote, " are very different in Reference to Property and Riches ; some parts subsist upon Mines and Cole, others upon Manufacture, some upon Corn, others upon the profits of Cattle, London and the Sea-Ports upon Exportation and Importation ; And it is not possible but that when those several things come to be regulated by Laws, the different parts of the Nation must necessarily

[1] Preface to " Holy Commonwealth."

[2] " Observations on Aristotle's Politiques touching forms of Government," E 665. Sidney also alludes to this criticism in his answer to Filmer's " Patriarcha," " Discourses," p. 451.

espouse very different interests." [1] This is an interesting if not a vital objection to democracy.

Of the individual proposals of " Oceana " the agrarian came in for the severest criticism. The other propositions were also condemned, rotation on the grounds that both houses would immediately repeal it, and the peculiar parliamentary system on the grounds that the lower chamber would not consent to be forbidden to initiate legislation.

But interest concentrated round Harrington's proposals for dealing with the land. These were open to the obvious comment that they were inconsistent with individualistic principles. It was argued that the restriction of property was a check to industry and honest labour. Wren pointed out that " the Liberty of disposing as a Man thinks fit of his own, is Essential to the Propriety we now dispute of." [2] Harrington had realised this and attempted to work out the details of the scheme in the spirit of Bentham and Mill. Wren either could not or did not want to follow the working of Harrington's mind, and criticised him for this very method. Although he was himself taking the point of view of the individualist in condemning the agrarian, he criticised Harrington for adopting the less drastic principle, based as it was on the view that State interference should be minimised and made as unobjectionable as possible, " No man shall be more than thus rich," instead of the more uncompromising Spartan principle, " Every man shall be thus poor." [3] In doing this he was both inconsistent and unintelligent.

The second criticism, which was commonly directed

" [1] Monarchy asserted or the state of Monarchicall and Popular Government : in vindication of the Considerations upon Mr Harrington's Oceana "
E 1853, p. 86.   [2] *Ibid.*, 146.
        [3] " Considerations . . . on Oceana," p. 81.

against the Agrarian, was based on different grounds. " Were the Agrarian . . . at once established," wrote Wren, " the Nobility would be so thoroughly plumed, that they would be just as strong of wing as Wild-fowle are in moulting-time." [1] Not only would the upper classes decline but they would desert the estates, which they had been compelled to divide, and flock to London. London, the abode of smoke, disease, and democracy, would grow in consequence to an undesirable size, and all the legislation which had been directed against its further growth would be undone.[2] This would be regrettable not only from the economic but also from the political point of view. It would result in the government of the country by the inhabitants of its capital.[3] The history of the next century was to prove the truth of this criticism in France.

The third criticism was based on economic grounds. It was argued that it was impossible to have a fixed agrarian because of the continual changing of the value of money. In addition to this, the maximum of property which it was lawful to hold would automatically get lower and lower until it resulted in complete levelling.[4] Harrington replied that this was unlikely, because the hired labourer, who earned £20 a year and kept his cow on the common, would be unwilling to exchange his position for that of a landowner in possession of land worth no more than £10 a year. But he was better versed in politics than economics, and could never satisfactorily refute this argument.

[1] "Considerations . . . on Oceana," p. 93.
[2] *Cf. ibid.* 86, and "Monarchy Asserted," pp. 149-50. *Cf.* Petty's frequent objections to the increase of London, and Evelyn's " Fumifugium," written in 1661.
[3] *Cf.* " A Discourse for a King and Parliament."
[4] "Considerations . . . on Oceana," p. 85; "Monarchy Asserted," pp. 149-50.

The theory on which the agrarian was based was also criticised. There was a certain amount of truth in Wren's contention that Harrington, in speaking of the balance of property, was simply using a new vocabulary to express the truism that " riches means power." [1]   But Harrington seems to have realised this, his purpose being rather to emphasise the peculiar power, which has undoubtedly been in the hands of the landowning classes in the course of history.

Such were the main objections urged against Harrington's theories. Many of them were sensible, but none of them vital. In view, however, of the actual development of English institutions, it should be pointed out that the system of rotation, necessitating as it does periodical elections, would have made the cabinet system impossible. Where legislative and executive functions are entirely confused, as in English local government, the period of membership must be limited by some such arrangement. And where legislative and executive functions are as much separated as they are in the United States, rotation could be extended to the House of Representatives without causing much alteration in the working of the constitution as a whole. But in the case of the subtle compromise between the separation and confusion of powers which is effected by the cabinet system, the result would be disastrous. It is true that the legislative body would be given more frequent opportunities for dismissing the executive ; but the executive would lose one of the greatest sources of its strength, the power to dissolve the legislative body at its will.

The tendency of the political theory of the Commonwealth, as indeed of much subsequent English political

[1] " Considerations . . . on Oceana," p. 14.

theory, was antagonistic to the actual line of development. Nevile, as will be shown later, was the only republican, and one of the few men who foresaw the possibility of something like that which actually happened. But the times in which he wrote were comparatively quiet. Harrington, writing in a period of general chaos, when it seemed that a new political era had dawned and what was good in mediæval conditions was forgotten in the condemnation of what was bad, not unnaturally made proposals which stood in need of modification when the old order was restored. His writings still influenced English political theory , but English institutions developed along other lines. To receive embodiment in practice the theories of the Commonwealth had to be conveyed to infant states across the Atlantic.

CHAPTER VI

§ I

WHEN it was certain that Charles II. would be restored,
Harrington retired into private life. Whether he had
given up all hopes of the ultimate establishment of
republican institutions or still thought that his prophecy
would be fulfilled and things would right themselves
automatically we cannot tell. In his retirement he
was not idle. People still came to discuss politics
with him, and he continued his literary work. One
of his visitors, an eminent royalist, persuaded him to
apply his theories to monarchy and draw up some
schemes which would assist the nation to settle down
quietly and quickly under the old régime. The scheme
which he drew up, submitted to several members of
Charles II.'s court, and finally handed over to one of
his ministers, has unfortunately not survived. The
other work in which he was engaged, although it is
nothing more than a fresh repetition of the old proposals
of " Oceana," was preserved in manuscript by one of
Harrington's sisters and passed on to Toland, who
published it for the first time in 1700. Called " A
System of Politics," it is the best and the clearest
of all Harrington's writings, and, though it is not
written in the picturesque form of a Utopia, it deserves
to be placed above the more famous " Oceana."

Harrington made no secret of the fact that he was

still engaged in republican compositions, and suffered for his audacity. On November 26th, 1661, he was committed to the Tower by the late chairman of his club, Sir William Poulteney, in company with his fellow-Rota-man, Major John Wildman, and the notorious Praisegod Barebones. These two men were implicated in a plot headed by an old Cromwellian officer, Colonel Salmon, which, following closely on Venner's Insurrection, created a great deal of excitement at the time. Cromwellians, supporters of the Long Parliament, Londoners, Purchasers, officers of the disbanded army, Independents, and Fifth Monarchy men were all concerned in the movement, these seven parties being represented by an inner council of twenty-one, which met in Bow Street and other parts of London. The aims of the conspirators are not quite clear. According to one account wholesale assassinations were arranged, and insurrections were to start in Shrewsbury, Coventry, and Bristol, to be followed by the return of all the republican exiles.[1] According to another account they merely attempted to get the right men elected for Parliament, and began with the members for the City of London, intending subsequently to petition Parliament for a preaching ministry and liberty of conscience, and to subdivide into local committees in view of extending the movement over the whole country.[2] Harrington was not unnaturally suspected of being implicated. Although his name did not occur in the report of the committee which was appointed by both houses to inquire into the whole plot, his friend Nevile had been selected for special mention,

---

[1] "Commons Journals," vii. 342. Kennet, "Register," p. 602. Parker, "History of his Own Time," ed. 1728, pp. 13 and 14. W. C. Abbott, "English Conspiracy and Dissent, 1660-1674," in the "American Historical Review" for April 1909, pp. 508 and 509.

[2] Cf. Toland's account in the Introduction to Harrington's "Works," xxxv.

and Wildman was known to be one of the leading
spirits. The burlesque decree of the Committee of
Safety of the Commonwealth of Oceana with its
reference to " the Politick casuists of the Coffee Club
in Bow Street," shows that Harrington at an earlier
date was in some way associated or connected with
the condemned locality.[1]   The rumour had also doubtless got about that he was anxious to continue the
meetings of his club.   Furthermore, he was known to
be writing a new account of his republican principles.
On the face of it it is improbable that Harrington
would take part in a conspiracy of this sort, particularly if the account given by the parliamentary
committee is the correct one.   His politics were too
academic for that.   But there was certainly an excuse
for ordering his arrest, and he had to pay for his activity
and notoriety during the year of anarchy.

For several weeks Harrington remained in the
Tower without trial.   His sisters worked hard to
procure his release.   One of them, being already known
to the King, obtained an audience with his majesty
and laid the case before him.   She urged that some
mistake must have been made, because the warrant
was issued against *Sir* James Harrington.   This
gentleman was a cousin of the author of " Oceana,"
who had served on most of the Councils of State under
the Commonwealth and Protectorate, and has since
been confused with his namesake by Noble in his
" Lives of the Regicides," by Froude, and by most
indexers.   Charles was by no means sympathetic,
but he ordered an examination to be conducted by
Harrington's kinsman, Lord Lauderdale, Sir George
Carteret, and Sir Edward Walker.   An account of
it was preserved by one of Harrington's sisters and

---

[1] This pamphlet is dated Nov. 12th, 1659

published by Toland.[1] Much to Sir George Carteret's discomfiture Harrington flatly denied that he had been implicated in the conspiracy, and pleaded that he had not seen Wildman or Barebones for some two years. He then proceeded to defend his action in continuing to write political works. He referred to the criticisms showered on him for meddling with politics in a private capacity, adding, " My Lord, there is not any public Person nor any Magistrat, that has written in the Politics worth a Button. All they that have been excellent in this way have been privat men, as privat men, my Lord, as myself. There is Plato, there is Aristotle, there is Livy, there is Machiavel." Plato lived under a democracy, but the others living under monarchical or oligarchical institutions were permitted to utter republican sentiments without molestation. His pleas were unavailing, and met with no response.

This examination did not serve to clear Harrington of his accusatiors. and he was no nearer to a public trial. But his sisters continued to do their best. On February 14th, Lady Ashton and Mrs Evelyn obtained permission to visit their brother. They were allowed to take a doctor to examine his health, and certain tenants, who refused to pay rent unless they saw their landlord sign their acquittances.[2] They found their brother in weak health owing to his imprisonment, and attempted to procure better treatment for him by a present of £50 to the Lieutenant of the Tower. But he was still no nearer to a public trial. He sent a petition to the King, asserting the innocent and peaceable nature of his past life. He also wrote a petition to Parliament, which he gave his sister ; but she could find no one willing to introduce it.

[1] It is also printed in Howell, " State Trials," v. 114 ff.
[2] "Cal. State Papers," Domestic Series, Feb. 14th, 1662.

Finally she moved for his Habeas Corpus. This was granted and duly served ; but the move was thwarted according to the custom which commonly prevailed before the passing of the Habeas Corpus Act in 1679, by removing the prisoner to a different gaol. The place chosen was a small rock off Plymouth called St Nicholas Island. Here he was still worse off. The narrowness of his quarters and the absence of fresh water aggravated his ill health. But a petition for his removal to the mainland was granted, his brother William, now a prosperous hemp merchant, and his uncle, Anthony Samuel, who was a distinguished architect, giving £5000 in bond for his good behaviour. At Plymouth he was better treated. He was allowed to take exercise on the Hoe, and he frequently received the hospitality of the deputy governor of the fort, whom he won over like everybody else by his charming conversation. But the state of his health grew more and more alarming. Too many doses of guiacum, given (some said) to prevent him from writing any more "Oceanas," others said to cure him of scurvy, brought on a curious form of madness. It was considered useless to keep him in confinement while he was in this condition, and he was finally released and moved to London.

The remainder of his life was spent in retirement.[1]

He returned to his old house "in the Little-Ambry (a faire house on the left hand) which lookes into the Deane's Yard in Westminster. In the upper story he had a pretty gallery, which looked into the yard . . . where he commonly dined and meditated and tooke his tobacco."[2] He was married late in life

---

[1] Wood's information that Harrington travelled on the Continent after the Restoration is not borne out by Aubrey or Toland.

[2] Aubrey, " Brief Lives," i. 233.

to his old love, the daughter of Sir Marmaduke Dorell of Buckinghamshire. He continued to see much of his friend Nevile; and he associated also with Sir Roger L'Estrange, the Tory censor, Sir Thomas Dolman, some time clerk to the Privy Council; Dr Pell, who was a man no less interested in foreign countries than mathematics; Andrew Marvell, who was drawn to Harrington by their common urbanity, and Aubrey, the recipient of the only letter written by Harrington which has survived. This letter would be of no particular interest otherwise. It runs as follows, and bears the date 1669.[1]

HONOUR'D SIR,—

It is very much agt my nature to fayle in anything might please a friend to whom I beare an hearty affection, but something, not worth giving account off, is nevertheless the reason why I cannot waite on ye according to my promise on Wensday night, for wh no fault of my owne, I yet humbly beg y^r excuse.—I am S^r

Yr affectionate

For his much   friend and servant,
honoured friend   J. HARRINGTON.
Mr AUBREY.

During these years of life in London Harrington's behaviour was rational enough in most things. But he constantly dwelt on a peculiar delusion, from which he had suffered since his illness at Plymouth. He imagined that he perspired the spirits of flies and bees, and he refused to believe his doctors when they put it down to a form of melancholy madness. Declaring

---

[1] A copy of the orignial, which is in the Bodleian, is in the British Museum, Egerton MSS. 2231, f. 187.

his belief in the Stoic philosophy, and adopting as his motto, " Vivere secundum Naturam," he wrote a treatise called " The Mechanics of Nature " (a fragment of which was published by Toland), to prove by the doctrine of the Anima Mundi that he was right in his philosophical contention.   He also tried an experiment which hardly helped to prove his sanity.   " He had," says Aubrey, " a timber *versatile* built in Mr Hart's garden (opposite to St James' Parke) to try the experiment.   He would turne it to the sun and sitt towards it ; then he had his fox-tayles there to chase away and massacre all the flies and bees that were to be found there and then shut his chassees.   Now this experiment was only to be tryed in warme weather, and some flies would lie so close in the cranies and the cloath (with which it was hung) that they would not presently show themselves.   A quarter of an hower after perhaps, a fly or two, or more, might be drawn out of ,the lurking holes by the warmth ; and then he would crye out, " Doe not you see it apparently that these come from me ? "

Harrington's health grew worse and worse.   By the year 1676 he had become a confirmed invalid.   His friend Nevile still visited him, faithful as ever.   On September 7th, 1677, he died.   He was buried in St Margaret's Westminster, on the south side of the altar, next to the grave of one whose writings and sympathies bore no small resemblance to his own, Sir Walter Raleigh.   Andrew Marvell wrote him an epitaph.   But it was feared that it might give offence.   The inscription which was set over his tomb was both dignified and unobjectionable :—

" Hic jacet Jacobus Harrington, Armiger (filius maximus natu Sapcotis Harrington de Rand, in Com. Linc. Equitis aurati et Janæ uxoris ejus, filiæ Gulielmi

Samuel de Upton in Com. Northamton. Militis) qui obiit septimo die Septembris, ætatis suæ sexagesimo sexto, anno Dom. 1677. Nec virtus, nec animi dotes (arrha licet æterni in animam amoris Dei) corruptione eximere queant corpus."

§ 2

This was the tragic end to a career which for at least one year can only be described as brilliant. But the ideas which were originated or advocated by Harrington lived on to exert a potent influence alike in England, America, and France. Before attempting to trace this influence, a few words must be said about the difficulty of any such undertaking.

It is generally realised that influences are of two kinds. There is the direct influence of the writer who attracts conscious imitators. There is the indirect influence which his ideas exert on those who do not imitate him. The mark which Plato has left in the world is not due only to those who have from time to time called themselves Platonists ; it must be ascribed also to the fact that his writings have been read by thousands of others in the impressionable years of life. The wider influence is often the more important, but it is of such a nature that it cannot possibly be gauged. Nothing can be done but to affirm its existence. The more direct influence on the other hand can be estimated with greater accuracy. But there are many obstacles in the path of one who attempts to perform the task. The writer, who is giving an account of a particular historical personality, is naturally apt to treat him in a sense as his hero, and to distort him in the process. Anxious to see his influence everywhere, he seizes hold of cases where a resemblance of idea suggests some connection, and forgets that it is possible for two people to draw from a common source without knowing each other or to reach the same conclusion by independent reasoning. Bias is inevitable, and it is almost impossible for him to speak with certainty unless actual reference is made to his hero or his hero's writings.

To apply what has been said to the case of Harrington, we cannot tell what his indirect influence has been. We know that " Oceana " soon became a classic and was one of the books on politics that people were supposed to have read. We may imagine that those who had attended the meetings of the Rota passed on something of what they had seen and heard, as they went out into the world. We can say no more. But in tracing his direct influence, in spite of the general tendency to overstate, we are in a peculiarly fortunate position.

His writings are not commonplace in idea or in diction : one of his theories is entirely original, and it is set forth in certain stereotyped phrases, which were coined by the author himself. And so, whenever we come across allusions to the balance of property or the connection of land and dominion, we are reasonably safe in attributing them without further question to the influence of " Oceana." With his other ideas which are rather less peculiar both in conception and presentation, more care must be taken. Bearing this in mind, we may proceed to trace Harrington's influence in the political literature of the seventeenth and eighteenth centuries.

The first person who may be noticed is Sir William Petty. In his visits to the Rota he is said to have " troubled Mr James Harrington with his arithemeticall proportion, reducing politie to numbers." [1] Never-

---

[1] Aubrey, " Brief Lives," ii. 148.

theless, the political economist appears to have been very much influenced by the political scientist. The opening words of Petty's most famous book—" that a small territory and even a few people may, by situation, trade and policy, be made equivalent to a greater ; and that convenience for shipping and water carriage do most eminently and fundamentally conduce thereunto " [1]—seem strongly to suggest that his study of economics was inspired by Harrington's " Oceana." It will be remembered that Harrington, in submitting his theory that power rests on property in land, excepted from his generalisation places like Holland and Genoa, where nearly all the wealth of the state came from commerce.[2] Petty seems to have taken Harrington's exceptional cases, developed his points, and shown that the exception is more important than the rule. The stress which he laid on the importance of commerce in his " Political Arithmetic " can be more readily understood, if it is considered as a criticism of Harrington's economics. If this is so, " Oceana " acquires a new importance as the inspiration of the first English book on political economy. In Petty's writings there are several curious resemblances to Harrington, which should be borne in mind in tracing this connection. Petty constantly referred to the problem of the growth of London and to the danger to monarchy of having " excessive and overgrown cities," but like Harrington he opposed any artificial restriction.[3] Like him he desired a redistribution of seats and equal shires, which would make the work of the statistician less troublesome.[4] Like him he clamoured for fewer priests and lawyers.[5] Finally

[1] " Economic Writings of Sir William Petty," C. H. Hull, i. 249.
[2] " Works," pp. 41, 245, 387.
[3] " Economic Writings of Sir William Petty," C. H. Hull, i. 40.
[4] Ibid. i. 301.　　　　　　　　　　[5] Ibid. i. 24, 27, 79, etc.

like him he wrote of the country's imperial aspirations in words which may now be read as prophetical. " The Government of New England (both civil and ecclesiastical) doth so differ from that of his Majesty's other Dominions, that 'tis hard to say what may be the consequences of it." [1]

Sir William Petty was the only member of the Rota Club (besides Nevile) to carry on Harrington's influence in the political literature of the Restoration period, but many other political writers of all shades of opinion bear traces of his influence. We may turn first to Sir William Temple. He was a political theorist of an extremely interesting type. He did not believe in doctrinaire politics, and for that reason condemned Harrington along with Plato and Hobbes.[2] Accepting the theory of paternalism as the origin of government, he ascribed its continuation to " the consent of the people or the greatest or strongest part of them." [3] But instead of making him a democrat, this doctrine caused him rather to lay stress on the conservative tendencies in human nature and to formulate the theory that government really rests on custom.[4] It seemed to him not to matter much whether a country has monarchical or republican institutions, as long as (i) people are acclimatised to them, (ii) the administration is good. So far not much resemblance to Harrington with his belief in exotic models and the importance of institutions is noticeable. Nevertheless certain of Temple's actual proposals bear traces of Harrington's influence. His scheme of 1678 for replacing the Privy Council by a body composed partly of royal officials and partly

---

[1] " Economic Writings of Sir William Petty," C. H. Hull, i. 298.
[2] In his essay, " Of Popular Discontents."
[3] " Miscellaneous Writings," i. 83.   [4] *Ibid.* pp. 54 and 83.

of members of Parliament is based on the political
experiments of the Commonwealth period, and it
suggests the type of Council dear to political romance.
That it was suggested in particular by " Oceana " may
be inferred from Temple's insistence on the wealth of its
members and his allusion to the theory of the balance
of property. " One chief regard," he wrote in his
" Memoirs," " necessary to this constitution was that
of the personal riches of this new Council ; which in
revenues of land or offices was found to amount to
about three hundred thousand pounds a year ; whereas
those of a House of Commons are seldom found to have
exceeded four hundred thousand. And authority is
observed much to follow land." [1]

The two proposals submitted in his essay, " Of
Popular Discontents," were doubtless due in part
to Harrington's influence. He here advised the com-
pilation of a register of all the lands in England and
Wales in order to give a greater security of tenure to
property-holders and to encourage foreigners to come
and settle in the country. And in order to check the
decline in the numbers of the nobility and gentry, he
suggested an act to limit dowries and make it illegal
for heiresses to marry other than younger sons. Proposals for registering the land and artificially propping
up the upper classes were frequently put forward by
the early Whigs. They were due partly to the conditions of the age that produced the Whig party,
partly to Dutch influence, but partly also to the
Harringtonian theories of the balance of property.

The influence of Harrington in Sidney's famous
" Discourses " on government cannot be definitely
traced. He started like Harrington with a firm belief
in Jewish, Greek, and Roman institutions, and he had

[1] Part iii. p. 16.

the same enthusiasm for the rule of laws. But he took refuge in the mixed form of government, which has attracted so many political writers and produced few ideas of interest beyond his proposal for the periodical revision of constitutions. For political sense this proposal compares favourably with Harrington's child-like belief in the incorruptibility of good institutions ; but Harrington's was an idea which was as important as Sidney's in the development of the theory of the written constitution.

Nevile, the other great republican writer of the period, not unnaturally reflects Harrington more closely, and his book, " Plato Redivivus," was in-cluded in the Dublin edition of Harrington's " Works." [1] The book was circulated privately in 1681, but it at-tracted enough notice to call forth at least two replies, the anonymous pamphlet, " Antidotum Britannicum," and Goddard's " Plato's Demon, or the State Physician Unmasked." It is impossible to give anything more than a brief account of the book.

The first point of importance is the refutation of the theory of the origin of government which had appeared the year before in Filmer's " Patriarcha," and the suggestion of an alternative, which was already meeting with acceptance from the Whigs and was destined to be made more famous by Locke. The theory that government was instituted for the pre-servation of property supplies an origin and explana-tion, real or imaginary, to the fact which Harrington was always asserting. When Nevile repeated the doctrine of the balance in these words, " Empire is founded upon Property ; force or fraud may alter a government ; but it is property that must found and eternise it," [2] he was using the word " found " in its

---

[1] See below, p. 146.   [2] "Plato Redivivus," p. 35.

double sense, and bringing a new argument to his
leader's proposition. But the value of Nevile's work
lies not in this new argument, but in the application
of Harrington's ideas to the problems of the Restoration period. Harrington had already prophesied that
a monarch would find his position difficult in England
because of the decline of the nobility and the purchase
of so much land by the lesser gentry and common
people.[1] Nevile now pointed out that this was an
adequate explanation of the difficulties which were
actually being experienced by Charles II. " The
natural part of our government, which is power," he
wrote, " is by means of property in the hands of the
people, while the artificial part, or the parchment, in
which the form of government is written remains the
same. . . . I do not affirm that there is no government
in the world but where rule is founded in property, but
I say there is no natural fixed government, but where
it is so and when it is otherwise, the people are perpetually complaining and the King in perpetual anxiety,
always in fear of his subjects and seeking new ways
to secure himself ; God having been so merciful to
mankind that he has made nothing safe for Princes
but what is Just and Honest." [2] Nevile saw two ways
of remedying this state of affairs : power could be
brought into correspondence with property, or property
with power. His republican sympathies led him to
adopt the former alternative. He therefore suggested
that the power of the King should be restricted in
certain directions. Influenced perhaps by Temple's

---

[1] Dryden ascribed the difficulties in Charles II.'s path to the same cause in
the lines—
              " Add, that the power for property allow'd
              Is mischievously seated in the crowd."
" Absalom and Achitophel," Part i. 777.
[2] " Plato Redivivus," p. 134.

scheme, he proposed, (i) to abolish the Privy Council and replace it by four new Councils elected by Parliament under a scheme of rotation to exercise in conjunction with the King the powers of making war and peace, controlling the militia, nominating to offices, and spending the national revenue ; (ii) to abolish the royal prerogative of creating peers and have them made in future by Act of Parliament ; (iii) to have annual Parliaments, and make a clear majority necessary for the election of members. These proposals, taken as a whole, were an interesting attempt to adapt republican ideas to the restored monarchy and to weaken the power of the Crown to an extent which would in some way correspond with its diminished resources. But each proposal has its point of special interest. The first, by compelling the King to exercise his power in conjunction with men approved by the nation, is an anticipation of one aspect of the cabinet system. The second is a further attempt to replace the power of the Crown by that of the Commons, rendered less objectionable by keeping the peerage hereditary and giving to existing peers a voice in the selection of their fellows. The third tends in the direction of proportional representation, and affords an additional proof of the confusion which characterised parliamentary elections in the seventeenth century, and the unrepresentative character of the members elected. " How can he be said to represent the country," runs Nevile's protest, " if not a fifth part have consented to his choice, as happens sometimes, and may do oftener, for where 7 or 8 stand for one vacant place, as I have known in our last long parliament, where the votes being set in columns, he who has had most votes, has not exceeded 400 of above 2000 who were present." [1]

[1] " Plato Redivivus," p. 249.

The method which Nevile suggested for introducing his reforms, has a modern ring about it. But it shows more optimism and sanity than knowledge of the Stuart character. He wished a conference to be arranged between King and Parliament, at which the King would be persuaded, that it was to the interest of monarchy to accept the existing economic conditions and relinquish certain of his powers. The revolution of 1688 was not so very different from this.

In Shaftesbury, Penn, and Locke, the three greatest prophets of civil and religious liberty in the age of the Restoration, the influence of Harrington is also marked. More will be said about them when the place of Harrington in American political theory is discussed, but there are certain considerations which must be noted at this point.

It is not easy to decide how much Shaftesbury borrowed from other people, because he wrote very little, and not much is now known of his ideas. Two facts, however, point to a connection between him and Harrington. Some time in the year 1681 a curious poem appeared under the title " Oceana and Britannia." It has been attributed to Marvell and printed in his collected works. But as Marvell died in 1678, and the poem bears unmistakable allusions to the Oxford Parliament of 1681, this must be a mistake. The authorship of the poem, however, is of no importance ; the interest lies in its contents. It was written to celebrate the salvation of the country from the Popish terror and the happy certainty of the Protestant Succession, brought about by the efforts of Shaftesbury. The form is allegorical, Harrington's names, Oceana, Marpesia, and Panopeia, being used for England, Scotland, and Ireland ; and the success of Shaftesbury's policy is connected with the revival of the Oceana vocabulary and ideas :

> " Propose, resolve, Agrarian, forty-one,
> Lycurgus, Brutus, Solon, Harrington."

The poem is very confused, and if there were no other considerations it would be natural to call it the work of some Harringtonian crank, who hoped to convert Shaftesbury to his way of thinking by merely asserting the fact. But the poem must not be taken by itself. In Shaftesbury's papers a pamphlet was found, which gave certain suggestions for reforming the electoral system.[1] All the householders in each parish were to elect 8 or 10 electors, who were to proceed to the county town to represent the county. The sheriff was to prepare a list of the men in his county that had reached the age of forty, were in possession of property of the value of £10,000, and were free from debt. In every county 7, 9, or 11 were to be chosen from this list by the assembled electors, and " to prevent the inconveniences of fear and favour," they were to register their votes by means of a dot placed against the names which they desired to support. The influence of Harrington is very clear in the ballot, the indirect election, and the qualifications for candidates. It is uncertain whether Shaftesbury was himself the author of the pamphlet, but in any case its discovery gives some support to the evidence of the poem. And knowing as we do that Shaftesbury stood for the rights of property and for civil and religious liberty, we are tempted to see some connection with Harrington.

An account of Penn will be given in another place. It will be sufficient here to call attention to some of

---

[1] " Some observations concerning the regulating of Elections for Parliament." In Somers' " Tracts," viii. 396.

the ideas which occur in what is not the least interesting of his works, his plan for a general European
union.[1] The definition of government as "an expedient against *Confusion* ; a restraint upon all *Disorder* ; Just Weights and an even *Balance* ; That one
may not injure another, nor himself by Intemperance,"
represents very well what Harrington tried to achieve
in many of his provisions for Oceana. In particular
the introduction of the ballot, "after the prudent and
commendable method of the Venetians," has been
met with before. His commendation of "the Knowledge of Government in general ; the particular constitutions of Europe and above all of his own country,"
as the statesman's best training ; his satirical remarks
on the wars of religion ; his argument that a European
federation would make travelling easy, all suggest
acquaintance with Harrington's writings. His idealism
and his general attitude towards democracy and
toleration would naturally bring him into sympathy
with one whose sentiments were so similar.

That Locke was influenced by the theory of the
balance of property is extremely probable. Like
Penn he was up at Oxford at the time when "Oceana"
was attracting a good deal of attention in academic
circles, and he doubtless read the book. He never
alludes to Harrington. But in the general reaction
against the scholasticism of the preceding age the
practice of making elaborate citations and references
became discredited, and writers like Locke went to
the other extreme and refused to acknowledge their
indebtedness to anyone at all.[2]

His most important work was, like Sidney's and

[1] "Memoirs of Hist. Soc. of Penn," vi. 268.
[2] The fragment on "The Roman Commonwealth," which is so full of
allusions to Harrington, has been wrongly ascribed to Locke by Fox Bourne.
See below, p. 178 and Appendix.

Nevile's, directed against Filmer's dangerous book.
Filmer was one of the leaders of thought in an age that
loved to speculate on the origin of government. It
was a somewhat unprofitable occupation, which
Harrington had kept clear of. But those who replied
to the author of the " Patriarcha " were compelled to
meet him on his own ground. And Locke devoted the
greater part of two long essays to what Nevile had
dismissed in a few pages. Filmer's contention that
government was paternal and that property, like
government, had descended from the father to the
eldest son from the creation of the world, called for
new definitions of the origin of property and government. Locke therefore asserted that the former is
derived from " the right a man has to use any of the
inferior creatures for the subsistence and comfort of
his life " ; therefore it cannot be confined to any single
man and his various descendants. In order to accept
Filmer's main thesis that " the ground and principles
of government depend on the original of property,"
he added that government exists for the preservation of property. In answering the extreme royalist
position, Locke had to use the same arguments that
Ireton had employed in answering the extreme democratic position. He went little further than Ireton
had gone in defending the rights of property, and,
though he gave a much more detailed account of the
origin of government than Nevile, he never brought
out the connection between the principles and the
facts, by which power rests in the land-owning classes,
as did the author of " Plato Redivivus." He was a
philosopher rather than a theorist, interested in ideas
rather than histories of government. His aims were
broader than those of Sidney and Nevile. With no
desire to provide a particular remedy for the evils of

the times, he wrote a positive apology for the Whig landowners. In setting out the philosophy of government by the gentry and the divine right of freeholders in its most perfect form, he supplemented Harrington's theory that property *does* rule by proving that it ought to, and gave an intellectual basis to the oligarchical rule which was to dominate the next century.

In saying that landowners ought to rule England Locke was justifying an accomplished fact which had been secured by the expulsion of James II. and reasserted in 1710 by the statute which, in the interests of liberty, imposed a property qualification on members of the House of Commons. The Great Rebellion, like the French Revolution, was largely a movement of the middle classes. The Revolution of 1688 was in no way inspired by the proletariat. One or two republicans took the opportunity to assert themselves ; one or two Harringtonian pamphlets appeared ; rotation was again suggested.[1] The Harringtonian scheme, which had been found among the Earl of Shaftesbury's papers, was published in 1689, and included in Somers' collection of tracts. Publicity was given to the experiment in the use of the ballot which had been made in the borough of Lymington. And a pamphlet from the pen of Harrington's friend, Marvell, in which the " Benefit of the Ballot " was explained, now saw the light.

In 1698 the erratic Whig writer and rational theologian, Toland, edited Milton's Prose Works, and in his preface hinted at the edition of Harrington, which he was to bring out two years later, by calling " Oceana " " for the practicableness, equality and completeness

---

[1] *Cf.* " Some remarks upon Government," State Tracts of William III., i. 161. " Now is the Time ; a scheme for a Commonwealth," Somers' " Tracts," x. 197.

of it the most perfect form of such a government that ever was delineated by any antient or modern pen."[1] But objections were made even to this. One cautious Whig, who has accepted all the oligarchic principles of " Oceana " and rejected the democratic proposi- tions, wrote as follows of its republication in 1700. " The author is Mr James Harrington, a person of very deep learning and observation ; but as this his book ' Oceana ' was calculated wholly for the meridian of a Commonwealth, I hold the reprinting of both his and Milton's works to be very ill done, at this time, and dangerous, especially to persons of unsound principles or judgment. I am sure the Royal family hath very little obligation to *the publisher*. Their projects for a Commonwealth are, God be praised for't, vanished ; what remains for every good Englishman to endeavour is, to maintain the Monarchy upon its antient basis, to render the crown what's its due, and since a mon- archy cannot subsist without a nobility, to have a just regard for and towards the persons and order of the House of Peers. For the Commons of England, of which I am myselfe a part and never hope to be other, I ever wish them a *just and rational Liberty*, both as to their consciences and properties. Great mistakes we have had on all sides among us, which have brought the severest calamities upon the nation. 'Tis now a full hundred years that we have been fluctuating *from one expedient to another*, and to my poor judgment all parties who have in their time been uppermost, have gone beside the marke."[2] People were becoming too comfortable under regulated monarchy to care about republicanism. Democracy was a thing of the past—and the future.

[1] " Life of Milton," p. 122.
[2] " Memorial to the Princess Sophia," p. 38.

The feeble cries of the doctrinaire republicans, as Toland pointed out, were not called forth by any hatred of monarchy. They were due to a dislike of the empirical politicians, whose views were expressed by Halifax, when he boasted of his hatred of " fundamentals."

The new edition of Harrington which inspired one further appeal for the introduction of the ballot [1] was widely read. We find it advertised in the State Tracts of William III. We hear of Shaftesbury's grandson sending two copies of the work to Holland.[2] We find large extracts from it in French, in the literary periodical which Bernard was producing at the Hague.[3] Harrington's economic interpretation of history began to be generally accepted. His account of Roman history may have been of no more than academic interest ; but nevertheless Walter Moyle, Bohemian, scholar, politician, thought it worth while to elaborate Harrington's position and show exactly how the change in the ownership of land had led Rome from limited monarchy to oligarchy and to democracy.[4] Harrington's treatment of English history in the sixteenth and seventeenth centuries was of more practical interest and was accepted by such important figures as Bolingbroke and Harley.[5] But the lessons which Harrington himself had drawn from it were almost reversed.

After the Restoration Nevile had followed his

[1] " An Enquiry into the Inconveniences of Public and the Advantages of Private Elections. With the method of the Ballott," 1701. The author's allusions to the theory of the balance of property show Harrington's influence no less than his proposals for electoral reform.

[2] " Letters of Locke, Sidney and Lord Shaftesbury," p. 71.

[3] " Les Nouvelles de la République des Lettres," Sept. 1900, pp. 243 ff.

[4] " The Roman Commonwealth." See Appendix.

[5] Cf. " Faults of both sides," Somers' "Tracts," xi. 678. Bolingbroke, " Works," i. 382-83.

master's lead and given up republicanism ; but in order to reconcile the economic and political conditions of the country, he had proposed that the King should be compelled to resign certain of his powers. Now the alternative way of achieving the same object, by giving the King greater material resources, was suggested.

The fullest and most elaborate proposal may be found in the " Memorial to the Princess Sophia," erroneously attributed to the pen of Bishop Burnet, and written in 1703. The author, who had been studying Toland's lately published edition of Harrington's " Works," was ready enough to accept all that had been written about the balance of property. He was conscious that in his own time the real wealth of England lay, not in the hands of the very rich nor in the hands of the people, but with the country gentlemen and merchants, who owned property ranging in value from £3000 to £5000 a year. This gave him cause for some alarm. " If they knew their own strength," he wrote in language which would be more naturally applied to the growth of the proletariat than to that of the middle classes, " I know not what single person on earth could govern them." However, he comforted himself by remembering their failure, when they actually held the reins of government at Cromwell's death, and dispelled his fears with the consoling thought, " God be thanked all are not cut out to be politicians. . . . I know the genius of the English nation too well, to believe that ever a commonwealth can by any possibility be settled among us. We *won't* be governed by one another, and therefore *must* have a sovereign to rule over us. Abuses from our Government may and have caused violent convulsions and alterations amongst us ; yet still we have allwayes settled upon the old bottom." [1] Realising the popular attachment to monarchy, he attempted to establish it on a securer economic basis. The three proposals which he made should be compared with those of Nevile. (i) He advised the King, by the use of thrift and by abstention from squandering the revenue on mistresses and favourites, to save sufficient money to make an annual purchase of a considerable amount of property, and by making this inalienable quietly to amass an estate which would be comparable with the old Crown lands. (ii) He proposed to secure the predominance of wealth in the second estate of the realm by restricting the gift of peerages to men having " amongst other pretentions an estate of at least £6000 per annum," and by compelling the new peers to register two-thirds of their estates as a barony descending to the heir to the title. (iii) He suggested that the Commons could be checked by the exercise of greater care in conferring knighthoods and baronetcies on men of mean origin, whether wealthy or not.[2]

In this way the theory, which had been used first as an argument for republicanism and afterwards as an argument for regulated monarchy, was now brought forward in support of an oligarchical tyranny. And ideas, which had prompted Harrington to propose measures for breaking up large estates, were now adopted by those who desired their formation.

Some twenty years later sentiments similar to those expressed by the author of the " Memorial," but more moderate, were again being voiced. Trenchard and Gordon, the Whig writers who published their weekly letter during the years 1721 and 1722, gave two letters

<hr>

[1] " Memorial to the Princess Sophia," pp. 31-32.
[2] *Ibid*. pp. 62-72.

to Harrington's theory.[1]   They accepted the doctrine that property is the first principle of power, and recognised the instability that follows the separation of political and economic power, but they committed themselves neither to Nevile's remedies nor to those of the author of the " Memorial."   " The great secret in Politics," they remarked, " is, nicely to watch and observe this Fluctuations and Change of natural Power, and to adjust the political to it by prudent Precautions and timely Remedies."   Their advice was to keep the nobles artificially strong by making commoners noble ; but if the people get unduly rich, the Crown and nobles must graciously admit them to power. At their own time, with property in the hands of the nobility and gentry, and power in the hands of the former by the constitution, and the latter by their " easy admittance into the legislature," they concluded (with a sentiment typical of the age), " we can preserve Liberty by no other establishment than what we have."

In 1737 two more editions of Harrington were issued, one in Dublin, which included " Plato Redivivus," one in London, which included several of Harrington's lesser tracts not printed in Toland's edition of 1700. Another appeared in 1747.   The Harringtonian theories were gradually becoming known, gradually being watered down, gradually becoming orthodox.   By the middle of the century their work was done.[2]   After they had been qualified and restated by Hume, on whom they exercised considerable influence, little was left to be said.[3]   Few would take the trouble to deny that " The Oceana is the only valuable model of a commonwealth that has yet been offered to the

---

[1] " Cato's Letters," iii. 150 and 159.
[2] Another edition was still to come—in 1771.
[3] *Cf.* Maitland, " Collected Papers," i. 22.

public." [1] Few cared, when Hume made an ideal commonwealth of his own, imitating closely Harrington's ideas and method, and relegating the ballot and rotation along with a form of federalism into the realm of academic ideals. Everyone would agree with sentiments like the following : " It is sufficiently understood that the opinion of right to property is of moment in all matters of government. A noted author has made property the foundation of all government ; and most of our political writers seem inclined to follow him in that particular. This is carrying the matter too far ; but still it must be owned that the opinion of right to property has a great influence in this subject." [2] And everyone would acknowledge with Hume that the two other great foundations of government are interest and custom. It was as safe to say that " a government may endure for several ages, though the balance of power and the balance of property do not coincide," as that " when the original constitution allows any share of power, though small, to an order of men who possess a large share of property, it is easy for them gradually to stretch their authority and bring the balance of power to coincide with that of property." [3]

His final statement of the case was given in the essay entitled, " Whether the British Government inclines more to absolute monarchy or to a Republic." He began as follows. " That property has a great influence on power cannot properly be denied ; but yet the general maxim that the balance of one depends on the balance of the other must be received with several limitations. It is evident that much less property in a single hand will be able to counterbalance

---

[1] Essay 16, " Idea of a perfect Commonwealth."
[2] Essay 4, " On the first principles of Government."   [3] *Ibid.*

a greater property in several ; not only because it is
difficult to make many persons combine in the same
views and measures, but because property, when
united, causes much greater dependence than the same
property, when dispersed." He explained this by
contrasting the power of the smaller capitalist with
the power of the millionaire, and applied what he had
said to the Crown in England, showing that, although
" the mere name of King commands little respect,"
his large revenue, derived from all sources, has given
him progressively increasing power.   He granted that
" in his closet " a man could form a better republic than
monarchy, but he was of opinion that monarchy was
more in accordance with the line of national development in England.   " Absolute monarchy," he concluded, " is the euthanasia of the British Constitution." [1]
" Though all kinds of government be improved in
modern times, yet monarchical government seems to
have made the greatest advances towards perfection.
It may now be affirmed of civilised monarchies
what was formerly said in praise of republics alone,
that they are a government of Laws, not of Men." [2]

During the eighteenth century England, with a
wonderful political instinct, was evolving new ideas
of government, which can be traced to no individual
statesman, practical or theoretical.   It was no age
for the doctrinaire.   Nevertheless the comfortable
rule of the King and the landed classes, which witnessed deeds of great brilliance, was promoted and
defended largely by a distorted version of Harrington's
theory of property.   And in the series of writers which
began with Locke and ended with Hume, Harrington's ideas found as large a place as those of any
other theorist.

[1] Essay 7.   [2] Essay 12, " Of Civil Liberty."

When a new class of political theorists arose to protest against this system, and the Utilitarians and Radicals became the leaders of English political thought, Harrington's more democratic ideas were again brought forward. Bentham agitated for the simplification of the law, started another campaign against priests and lawyers, and proposed annual Parliaments, with re-stricted re-eligibility of members, and quadrennial elections of the premier. Short popular Parliaments and the abolition of the rights of primogeniture figured in the programme of all the Radicals, and many ideas which had been associated with republicanism again appeared. In 1835 rotation was adopted for local government. The ideas were Harrington's, but there is no need to ascribe their revival to any in-fluence of his—with one exception.

The agitation for the ballot since the dissolution of the Rota had been feeble and spasmodic. Secret voting had been adopted for the Royal Society, the Bank of England, and various Clubs and Companies as a matter of course, but in national politics it was still regarded with suspicion. In 1662 Middleton's Billeting Act introduced secret voting in Scotland for the disqualification of certain government officials. In 1677 the borough of Lymington made unsuccessful experiments in the use of the ballot for parliamentary elections. In 1707 the disputed election at Ashburton was decided by the coloured balls and boxes which the Commons had purchased for the purpose. In 1710 the freeholders of Yorkshire and Middlesex were given permission to elect their registers by secret vote. And during the last years of the seventeenth century, and with varying regularity during the eighteenth century, committees of the Lords and Commons were chosen by written votes placed in glasses. But the most important attempts to introduce the ballot met with failure. The proposals for its general use at elections, which were made in 1695 and 1710, were no more successful than Fletcher of Saltoun's similar suggestion in Scotland. And the motion brought forward in 1693 to introduce the ballot into the procedure of the Lords was likewise rejected.[1]

But no genuine agitation was started till Bentham and the Radicals added it to their proposals for universal suffrage. The movement reached its height when Grote, the author of the well-known history of Greece, was returned in 1832 as member for the City of London. In his election address he asserted that, " without the ballot, free and conscientious voting is unattainable," and after his election he devoted all his energies to securing its introduction in England. He distributed model ballot boxes over the country ; in 1833, 1835, 1838, and 1839 he brought in motions ; and in 1836 and 1837 bills providing for its use at parliamentary elections. But his persistence was not rewarded. The " Times " called him " chimerical," and the House and the nation at large failed to respond to his enthusiastic appeals Had Grote lived one year longer than he did he would have seen that his efforts had not been really vain. In 1872 the ballot became the statutory method of electing members of Parliament ; and it is now apparent that its introduction was due to him more than any other single person.

We know from the way in which Harrington was quoted and used to supply mottoes for the title-pages of the pamphlets of the time that " Oceana " was even then the *locus classicus* in the literature of the ballot. But there is a much more striking proof of its connec-

---

[1] This section is based on the Lords' and Commons' Journals, and on an article in the " Political Science Quarterly," vol. iii., on " The Ballot in England."

tion with the movement. In the manuscript department of the British Museum there is an unpublished critical essay on " Oceana " by Grote, which shows a very careful study of the book It need not be contended that Grote's enthusiasm for the ballot was entirely or mainly due to reading Harrington. But with such evidence it is reasonable to suppose that " Oceana " was a factor in the case. Thus, however academic its influence may have been, the book deserves a place in the history of the ballot in England. It would have come eventually if Harrington had never been read and if Grote had never been born. But the fact remains that Grote was born and that he studied Harrington. Therefore " Oceana " must be put down as one of the influences to which the introduction of the ballot was directly due, and one concrete illustration of the power of theoretical writings must be acknowledged.

Harrington's influence in England was thus twofold. He helped to justify the rule of property on lines quite contrary to his own. He helped to secure the acceptance of the ballot. But before the days of Grote " Oceana " had played a rôle in America and France, which was far more important than the rôle it played in England.

CHAPTER VII

HARRINGTON'S INFLUENCE IN AMERICA DURING THE SEVENTEENTH CENTURY

§ 1

No one who has studied Harrington's writings can help being struck by the resemblance between the political ideas expressed there and those that have been successfully put into practice in America. Again and again one is tempted to substitute the name America for Oceana and spell his new England with a capital N. The written constitution, the unlimited extension of the elective principle, and the separation of the three functions of government lie at the root of American political theory ; the equal division of property among the children is one of the most far-reaching social and political factors in the United States ; the principle of indirect election, though now discredited, has been employed since the formation of the Union. Short tenure of power, the multiplication of offices, the system of checks and balances, rotation, the ballot, the use of petitions, the popular ratification of constitutional legislation, the special machinery for guarding the constitution, religious liberty, popular education—all these things play their part in America. The only important proposal made in " Oceana " which has not survived is the proposal to separate the functions of debate and result. And even this has been more nearly realised in America than in England. For in the first place the result of the extensive employment of Committees in Congress, by which the majority of measures are handed over to a picked section of members for discussion and voted on by the whole body with the minimum of debate, has been virtually to separate the debating and the voting in the making of statutes.   In the second place the normal method of amending the constitution by which Congress proposes the desired change and the State legislatures ratify or reject the proposal, places the right of initiating and the right of passing into law in different bodies.

Furthermore, there are certain traits in the American character like the cosmopolitan spirit, the belief in travel, the capacity for selecting what is valuable in foreign countries, and even the love of Venice, which remind us of Harrington's affinity with America.   And his sympathetic prophecy of American independence, and the picture which he drew of the founder of " Oceana " passing, like Washington at the completion of his work, into honourable retirement, help us to realise that Harrington was in a certain sense made of the same stuff as the modern American.   In short it may be said that Harrington, like Herodotus, was an American before the American type was evolved.

But the similarity between American ideas and those of Harrington is not only due to coincidence. It should be borne in mind that when Harrington was at the height of his publicity the colonies of Virginia, Maryland, Massachusetts, Rhode Island, and Connecticut had already been brought into existence, and other colonies were founded shortly after.   Many of the early settlers had breathed the same political atmosphere as Harrington, had gone to the same university, and had read the books that he had read. Some of them, like him, had spent a portion of their lives in the Netherlands, where they came into contact with men of many countries   If they had not been in Italy themselves, they had met men who had been there, and they had heard the praise of the Italian republics sung. They had taken part in the government of their town at home, and some of them had been brought up in the democratic environment of the gild and trading company. They had been moulded by the influences which moulded Harrington.

From this point of view a study of Harrington's life and writings is not without value to American history. We focus our gaze on one man. In him we see the blending of English, Dutch, Italian, Greek, Roman, Jewish ideas ; the influence of the town, the gild, the company, the college, the church. And as we realise how many factors played a part in the conception of the state of Oceana, we begin to realise also the foundations on which the United States have been built. The Constitution was not thought out round a table in Philadelphia. The men who debated there discovered a way to unite a disunited people under a common government, and produced the first great example of the modern federal state ; but the ideas on which they founded the Constitution were independent of federalism. The fundamental doctrines of American democracy had been implanted in America for over a century, and before they were ever planted in America they were being tested in the countries and institutions to which reference has been made. American historians have been inclined to take a narrow view of their national history ; by over-concentration they fail to see the whole truth. The one writer who has trod outside the beaten paths has spoilt his work by not restraining his bitterness towards England, and by overstating his Dutch point of view.[1] An impartial study of the influences which produced Harrington serve to illustrate in some degree the origin

[1] Campbell, " The Puritan in England, Holland and America."

of the Constitution of the United States. The ideals that are found in both are drawn to a great extent from identical sources.

But we must go further than this. Not only was there the same background to " Oceana " and the ideas that took root in America. The book was itself read at two different periods in American history, and the prophetic jests of the journalists, who suggested that the theories of the Rota-men should find a home across the Atlantic, were more shrewd than they themselves knew.

Of the two periods in which the direct influence of Harrington is to be traced, the first is that of the Restoration in England. " Oceana " was published in 1656. Between 1660 and 1688 Carolina, New Jersey, and Pennsylvania were planted.

All three were what are called proprietary colonies. The proprietary colonies differed in two respects from the colonies of New England. The latter were in the first place little theocracies, in which affairs of State and Church were closely entwined and civil matters were determined ecclesiastically. In the second place they started as corporations, and gradually achieved self-government by the transference of authority from England to the seat of the corporation's activity. The proprietary colonies, on the other hand, had primarily secular interests, and constitutions were made for them at definite times by definite individuals, who had an external and separate existence. In this way it was much more easy to introduce a particular scheme into a proprietary colony. For the proprietors had full power to govern their lands as they pleased, provided that they kept within the terms of the charter which they were granted. The proprietors of the colonies in question were mostly serious and educated men. They had lived through a period of political changes and experiments, and they set about their tasks with full consciousness of their meaning and importance. They consulted their friends, they employed the most famous lawyers of the day to assist them, and they made use of the lessons that could be learned from the colonies that had been previously planted. And, living as they did in an age which set great store by the opinions of scholars, they consulted political writings with interest.

It was therefore highly probable that " Oceana " would be utilised. It was a book that for four years, from 1656 to 1660, had created a great stir. It had been much discussed at Oxford. Its author for one year at least had enjoyed great publicity in London. He had attracted crowds to his club. He knew many of the leading men of his day, and if he was generally looked on as a crank, he received the advertisement which is always the crank's portion. The book itself was written in a form which would be helpful to a person designing a frame of government. It was no abstract work on government. It was sufficiently imaginative to appeal to the idealist, and sufficiently concrete to appeal to the lawyer. Its doctrines were capable of either an aristocratic or a democratic interpretation. It was not theocratic in tone, and it contained the doctrines of religious liberty which the proprietors considered necessary for their plantations.

On à priori grounds it is reasonable to suppose that the book was referred to by the framers of the constitutions in question. Proof, however, is afforded by independent evidence, which must now be examined.

§ 2

The first of these colonies to be planted was Carolina. The charter given to the eight proprietors in 1663 and renewed in 1665 was itself liberal, and the government that was set up was of a democratic nature. A governor was chosen by a scheme of indirect election, and great power was given to a popularly elected assembly. For the new plantation which was proposed at Cape Florida in 1667 similar concessions were advertised ; and, to prevent the assumption of arbitrary power, the governor was not permitted to hold office for two consecutive terms ; he was " to rule for three years and then learn to obey." [1] In 1669 this arrangement, which was simple and in many ways admirable, was suddenly reversed. The proprietors, declaring that they wished to avoid the erection of a " numerous democracy," agreed upon the curious aristocratic scheme known as the Fundamental Constitutions.

The new system was based upon a very elaborate division of the people into classes determined by the amount of land they held. The whole territory was to be divided in such a way that the proprietors should have one-fifth, the hereditary nobility one-fifth, and the people three-fifths " that so in setting out, and planting the lands, the balance of the government may be preserved." At the top of the scale were the proprietors. Below them were the hereditary order of the landgraves, with inalienable estates of exactly 48,000 acres each ; below them the hereditary order of the caciques, with estates of exactly half this amount ; and below them the commons—first the lords of the manor, possessing anything from 3000 to 12,000 acres ;

[1] "Cal. State Papers," Colonial Series, 1675-76, No. 377.

next the freeholders, who needed 500 acres to be
eligible for parliament, and 50 acres to be enfranchised ;
finally the serfs or leet-men, with 10 acres but without
freedom.

The whole scheme was built up round the ownership of land.   The man who lost his land lost his title.
A property qualification was attached to every office.
Executive power was solely in the arbitrary hands of
the proprietors.   The judicial power they shared with
representatives of the landed nobility and the more
wealthy commoners, who were elected in each case
indirectly for life.   The legislative power was divided
between two bodies, a grand council of 50, of whom
only 14 could be said in any way to represent
the people, and a parliament, in which proprietors,
landgraves, and caciques sat in virtue of their property
together with a nearly equal number of wealthy
commoners.   All measures were to be proposed in the
council and decided in the parliament.

Complete toleration in matters of religion was continued ; marriage was to be a civil rite ; everybody
was to undergo military training ; and it was expressly
stated that the ballot should be used at elections.

In England the opinion was held that the constitution would last for ever.[1]   The proprietors at any rate
thought so ; for they set their seals to a sacred and
unalterable instrument which was to be " perpetually
established " in the colony.   To ensure a proper knowledge of the terms of the constitution, provision was
made for it to be read and sworn to in every parliament.
To prevent possible alteration, ordinary and constitutional legislation were distinguished, and power was
given to each of the four orders to veto unconstitutional
proposals.   To discourage the tampering influence of

[1] Dixon, " Life of William Penn," p. 191.

the legal mind, comments or expositions of the law were forbidden, and no man might plead a cause for money. To keep the government simple, laws were to expire automatically at the end of sixty years.

It will be seen at a glance that this frame of government is based entirely on the principle that power follows property. The principle is applied in the most aristocratic way. The equal division of property among the children is referred to only to be rejected. In order to ensure that the government may not become democratic, the right of proposing laws is reserved for the great landowners, who are made office-holders in virtue of being landowners. And in order to keep the class of great landowners in existence, property was made inalienable.

Unfortunately the author of the scheme is unknown. It has long been held that Locke framed it for his friend Shaftesbury. Des Maizeaux, who published "A collection of several pieces by Mr John Locke" in 1720, included the Constitution in his collection on the authority of a friend of his, who stated that it had been given him by Locke as a work of his own. Defoe followed Des Maizeaux. But the value of Des Maizeaux's assertion is seriously weakened by the fact that he printed in this same collection a work which is now known not to have been written by Locke. For other reasons it is not altogether probable that a little-known man, who was shy of publishing any books in his youth, would undertake the work.[1]

The composition has also been attributed to Shaftesbury. Oldmixon, in his early history of the British Empire in America, held this view on the ground that he was "the only one (of the proprietors) that could be suspected of having the least inclination to favour

[1] Cf. Fox Bourne, "Life of Locke," i. 239.

the dissenters."[1]   This was certainly an insufficient ground.   But it must be acknowledged that the ideas expressed are generally quite in keeping with what we know of Shaftesbury's aristocratic views.

Whether Shaftesbury or Locke was the principal author of the scheme, it seems clear that it was a deliberate attempt to put into practice " Oceana," divested of some of its democratic features.   We have the doctrine of the balance.   We have the same sort of fantastic nomenclature.   We have the same two chambers, one to propose and one to make laws, with the important difference that here the popular element in the upper chamber is much smaller.   We have the ballot, the provisions directed against lawyers, the theory of the incorruptibility of good governments, and other things which have already been met with in " Oceana."   It has been shown that Locke and Shaftesbury were probably acquainted with Harrington's work.[2]   It may be added that three other of the proprietors were in some way connected with Harrington.   The Earl of Craven was in command of the regiment in which Harrington had served during his stay in the Netherlands, and was the life-long friend of the Princess Elizabeth, who had been so much attracted by Harrington.   Sir George Carteret had been one of the judges in Harrington's trial, and his reluctance to find him guilty had been most noticeable.   The Duke of Albemarle, as General Monk, had been accused of Harringtonian tendencies.   There is no reason to suppose that any of these three were connected with the framing of the measure, but it is not unreasonable to imagine that they would fall in with a scheme that was suggested by Harrington's writings.

The scheme, which was in many ways more fantastic

[1] First edit., p. 332.   [2] Above, pp. 137-41.

than its model, enjoyed much fame. " Empires," wrote an admirer of Shaftesbury's, " will be ambitious of subjection to the noble government, which deep wisdom has projected for Carolina."[1] Shaftesbury himself spoke of it as " the best concessions issued in any colonies."[2] But fame was to be its only portion. It never enjoyed anything but a partial existence. Locke and a few others were made landgraves, and the proprietors still held to their ideas of the balance of property. In the Fundamental Constitutions they had made references to the theory ; in their " Temporary Agrarian Laws " of June 1674, they still asserted that " the whole foundation of the government is settled on a right and equal distribution of land " ; and in 1698 property was still to be the foundation of " all power and dominion " in Carolina. A tiny council was formed to propose what legislation might be needed, and a tiny parliament was called to deal with their proposals. But continued disputes arose. The popular assembly clamoured for greater power, which was given them in 1682. And finally in 1693 an equal right of initiating legislation was given to both houses.

The early history of the colony is a history of struggles and disputes. For twenty-nine years the proprietors kept on sending out different instructions and constitutions, all of them based on the scheme of 1669. After 1698 they wearied of their work. In 1719 Carolina became a royal province, and the first attempt to realise " Oceana " failed.

§ 3

The next colony in which an attempt was made to put into working the ideas of " Oceana " was New

[1] Bancroft, " History of the United States," i. 420.
[2] Osgood, " The American Colonies in the Seventeenth Century," ii. 208.

Jersey. The colony had been founded in 1664 ; and
its two proprietors, Lord Berkeley and Sir George
Carteret, had given it a business-like and democractic
constitution.   In 1676 the division of the colony was
made, and Penn acquired an interest in the western
section, where he determined to begin his political
experiments.   In the words of one of his many biog-
raphers, " Full of his old dreams of a model state and
fresh from the study of Harrington and More, he was
not content to carry on the government of the province,
as he found it, simply as a commercial venture, and
without regard to the working out of great ideas." [1]
In 1676 a frame of government was drawn up, probably
by Penn himself,[2] in which a combination of democracy
and toleration was attempted.

The constitution is interesting especially for three
of its provisions, all of which may be paralleled from,
if they were not suggested by, Harrington's writings.[3]
In the first place, the land was to be divided up care-
fully on a decimal system.   In the second place, particular stress was laid on the fundamental nature of
the constitution.   It was to be posted up in various
parts of the province and solemnly read at stated
intervals.   The legislature was forbidden, in language
of great emphasis, to introduce alterations or to make
laws contrary to its provisions.   And " seven honest
and reputable persons " might accuse of treason
anyone who attempted so to do.   In no set of concessions had the sanctity of the written constitution
been so jealously guarded.   In the third place, as in
Carolina, balloting " boxes " or " trunks " were to
be used at elections " for the prevention of partiality,

[1] Dixon, " History of William Penn," p. 145.
[2] Pennsylvania Hist. Soc. " Magazine of History," v. 312.
[3] It is printed in the " New Jersey Archives," i. 241 ff.

and whereby every man may freely choose according to his own judgment and honest intention." Secret voting was in use in the New England colonies ; but there the term that was employed was " papers " and not ballot.[1] The term " ballot " had been brought into common use by Harrington, and Chalmers, the trustworthy author of " Political Annals," attributes its introduction in the proprietary colonies to his influence.[2]

After Sir George Carteret's death in 1679 Penn also acquired an interest in the eastern section of the province, becoming one of the 24 proprietors who governed the province from 1682. The Fundamental Constitutions which they agreed upon in 1683 were perhaps the most interesting and complete of all the attempts to introduce Oceana in the colonies.[3]

The province was to be administered by a governor, the governor's council, and a grand council. The governor was to be elected by the proprietors for three years, and no man might serve for two consecutive terms. His council was to consist of the 24 proprietors, or their proxies, and 12 free-men chosen by lot from the Grand Council. It had no legislative power, and for its administrative duties it was to be divided into committees. The Grand Council was to consist of the 24 proprietors and 72 others elected on a property qualification. The 72 were divided into three series, and the third that retired each year were declared ineligible for two years. Toleration and the civil form of marriage were secured. Provisions were made for " avoiding innumerable multitude of Statutes." The fundamentals of the constitution were to be jealously protected. And the purity of elections was to be maintained by the employment of the lot at certain

---

[1] C. F. Bishop, " Colonial Elections," p. 166.
[2] " Political Annals," p. 642.
[3] It is printed in the " New Jersey Archives," i. 395 ff.

stages of the electoral process. Finally certain regulations were made for keeping " the just Ballance both of the Proprietors among themselves and betwixt them and the people." In the first place, none of the 24 proprietors was allowed to possess more than " one four and twentieth part of the country." In the second place, any proprietor failing to retain land amounting to one ninety-sixth part of the whole province was to forfeit his " right of government," apparently on the calculation that it is the correct proportion to give power in an assembly of 96. His place was to be filled by the remaining proprietors, who were to elect by ballot someone who had the requisite ninety-sixth, or if this were impossible, someone who had property large enough " to carry the character of the government."

It is not known who was primarily responsible for the introduction of this scheme, but it is probable that many of the provisions were due to Penn. Evidence of his acquaintance with " Oceana " will be given in the section following. It is enough here to point out that it bears a striking resemblance to the Carolinan scheme, and is almost an arithmetical application of Harrington's theory of the balance of property. When the colony was " boomed " in Scotland in 1685, it was commended, in words that might have come from Harrington's own pen, for providing " that *Dominion* may follow *Property*, and the inconveniency of a *Beggarly Nobility* and *Gentry* may be avoided." [1] In other respects its similarity to the provisions of " Oceana " is so remarkable that it is sufficient just to mention the fact.

The third of the colonies which are being considered, is the one which was nearest to Penn's heart, Penn-

---

[1] " The Model of the Government of the Province of New Jersey," Edinburgh, 1685.

sylvania. But before its constitution is discussed, a few words must be said about its founder.

William Penn is one of the most interesting characters of the seventeenth century. Much has been written about him, and the estimates of his importance have been various. Montesquieu compared him with Lycurgus. Jefferson called him " the greatest lawgiver the world has produced ; the first in either ancient or modern times, who laid the foundations of Government in the pure and unadulterated principle of peace, of reason and of right." [1] Macaulay disparaged him. It was general to place him on the same plane as Roger Williams, the founder of Rhode Island. The present age is again beginning to consider him a very great man. If Franklin was the greatest American of the eighteenth century, Penn was the greatest American of the seventeenth century, the most important of all the pioneers of colonisation. It is fitting that in the entrance of Independence Hall words which he wrote in the preamble of the constitution of Pennsylvania should be coupled with words taken from the Declaration of Independence to express the ideals on which the United States are founded.

Certain aspects of his character must be noticed in attempting to estimate the influence which Harrington had over him. Son of an admiral in the British Navy, he was not marked by the austerity and dourness of the typical Puritan. He was characterised by a friend as " mighty lively but with innocence," [2] and Pepys at one period of his life considered him quite " a modish person." There were certain amusements that he disapproved of and made illegal in his colony ; but he was always fond of athletics. He was a skilful fencer. In one of his visits to the Indians he won their unending

[1] Hazard, " Register," xvi. 48. [2] Aubrey, " Brief Lives," ii. 132.

respect by entering for the high jump and beating the field. He had studied at Paris as well as Oxford. He had travelled considerably on the continent. He moved in royal circles. He was an intimate friend of James II. and William III. He was presented at the Court of Louis XIV. He met the Czar. In spite of his aristocratic birth and environment he was a republican. There were not a few republicans in England in the seventeenth century, but Penn belonged to the rarer and less uncompromising type. He was one of those who had been made democratic by reading and travel, but were sufficiently wise and tolerant to be able to keep on terms of friendship with opponents and even with kings.

Although a man of moderation and practical ability, Penn was at the same time essentially an idealist. To realise this one has only to look at the picture which was painted of him at the age of twenty-two. One sees there the face of the man who dreams dreams. All through his life this trait can be noticed. At the age of seventeen he was suddenly converted to a mystical form of Puritanism. In the same year he first thought of the possibility of a newer and broader life in America. "I had," he wrote in 1681, "an opening of joy as to these parts in the year 1661, at Oxford, twenty years ago." [1] In 1682 he crossed the ocean. To the English sailor the perils of the Atlantic were a part of the day's work, and the land on the other side was just like any foreign country. But to the educated man the voyage was a different matter ; and it needed courage and imagination even for an admiral's son to make it. His dealings with the Indians, his plan for the union of the American colonies, his scheme for a general European federation, his

---

[1] " Pennsylvania Hist. Soc. Memoirs," i. 209.

advocacy of peace—all these things are evidence of the same idealistic spirit.

As what we may call a " gentlemanly republican," and as idealist it is extremely probable that Penn would be attracted by one who in so many ways resembled him. It is difficult to believe that a republican did not read what was one of the principal contributions to the republican literature of the time. It is probable that an idealist would look into what purported to be an ideal state. He may have read " Oceana " at Oxford in 1660 or 1661, when his mind first turned in the direction of America. He may have talked about Harrington with Sir W. Petty and Aubrey, the two members of the Rota, whom he knew. It is likely that he read " Plato Redivivus." For it was published in the same year that the constitution was being designed ; and the revival of interest in Harrington was at the same time being celebrated in verse. His opportunities for acquiring a knowledge of Harrington's ideas were peculiar, and the probability that he did so was great.

What then were the main provisions of the constitution which was framed for Pennsylvania ? Penn as proprietor claimed no special power. He had been unwilling that the name of the colony should suggest his own name. And he now refused any privilege beyond a double vote in the legislative body. " For the matters of liberty and privilege," he wrote, " I propose that which is extraordinary and to leave myself and successors no power of doing mischief ; so that the will of one man may not hinder the good of the whole country." Like the imaginary Cromwell of " Oceana," and like Washington, Penn wished to efface himself for the public good. The power which he denied himself was to be in the hands of two chambers.   The Provincial Council was to consist of seventy-two members, of whom a third was elected annually for three years.   Members were to be ineligible for re-election for one year after their retirement in order to leave room for new office-holders, " that so all may be fitted for government and have experience of the care and burden of it."   They were to propose all legislation and have their measures affixed in public thirty days before the meeting of the Assembly.[1]   For specialised work they were to be divided into four committees of eighteen, each committee being composed of six new members, six members of two years' standing, and six members of three years' standing.   The four committees were to supervise plantations, justice, trade, and education respectively.   The Assembly was to be elected annually, and was to consist of two hundred members.   Their duties were to approve or reject the proposals of the Council.   They were allowed to debate for a certain length of time and to propose amendments, but their primary function was that of voting on the Council's proposals.   Their votes, as the votes of those who elected them, were to be given by ballot.   Executive officers were generally to be appointed by the governor from a double set of names sent up by the Council or the Assembly.   No person was " to enjoy more than one public office at one time."   There was to be complete toleration, and marriage was to be a civil rite.

The ownership of land was still made necessary for any participation in the government, but the constitution was much more democratic than those of the other proprietary colonies.[2]   And in order that

---

[1] Six weeks was the period of promulgation in Oceana.   *Cf.* " Oceana," p. 155.

[2] In reference to the provisions about land and toleration, Oldmixon's

it might so remain no alteration was to be made without the consent of six-sevenths of the members of the Council and the Assembly.

It is at once apparent that nearly all the main ideas of " Oceana " are again reproduced here. The similarity is so striking that one is tempted to dub the thing a mere plagiarism.

But it ought not to be forgotten that Penn was himself a traveller, nearly as familiar with the Continent as Harrington. It is quite possible that he took the provisions of his constitution from Continental sources and not indirectly through " Oceana." Oldmixon in fact states that " the frame of government . . . was founded on what was excellent in the best German and other foreign constitutions of commonwealths." For reasons that will now be shown it seems more probable that Oceana was his inspiration.

There are certain documents in the possession of the Pennsylvania Historical Society which throw some light on the history of the constitution. They consist of a series of preliminary drafts of frames of government for the colony in many handwritings. Some are nothing but legal documents. Others are criticisms of Penn's schemes. Some are skeleton constitutions drawn out with admirable neatness on a single sheet so that the eye can take in the whole scheme at a glance. Some are written out in full detail. A few are fragmentary. All have passed through Penn's hands and have been annotated in his handwriting. They show in unmistakable manner the trouble which Penn took over his " holy experiment," his " free colony for all mankind."

curious phrase should be noted, " Mr Penn had all the laws so framed that no difference was made in opinion where property made no difference." " British Empire in America," first edit., p. 170.

The attitude in which he approached his task is shown in the letter which he wrote to James Harrison. " I eyed the Lord in obtaining it," he wrote with reference to the grant, " and more was I drawn inward to look at him, and to owe it to his hand and power than to any other way. I have so obtained it, and desire to keep it that I may not be unworthy of his love, but do that which may answer his kind providence, and serve his truth and people, that an example may be set to the nations."

He consequently spent much of his time during the years 1681 and 1682 in designing the most perfect constitution possible for his colony. He consulted his friends. He received help from the high-minded Algernon Sidney. He sought the advice of his trust-worthy Dutch agent, Benjamin Furly, a man who was acquainted with most of the Englishmen of the day, who were interested in the causes of liberty and tolera-tion. A Councillor Bamfield lent his counsel. A certain T. R. gave helpful suggestions. The informal arguments and conversations, which Penn had with his friends, can never now be known. We can only guess them from the cases in which it was necessary to resort to correspondence. For correspondence is only used where interviews are impossible. The legal aspect of the work was entrusted to the very best lawyers of the day, "that great lawyer, Sir Will Jones, and other famous men of the long robe,"[1] of whose names the only one that has survived is that of Darnall.

In short, Penn seems to have spared himself no trouble to make his experiment a success. The con-stitution was not the work of a solitary amateur, who scorned assistance. It was rather a composite pro-

---

[1] Oldmixon, " British Empire in America," p. 170.

duction, comparable to the constitution framed a century later for the United States, the outcome of many compromises and many suggestions.

It is impossible with the existing evidence to reconstruct with certainty the stages through which the constitution passed before it assumed its final form. At an early period in the discussions there were two very different schemes that were being sent out for approval. One was of a democratic, one of an aristocratic nature.

The democratic one, bearing the title of " The Old or first 24 Constitutions," which was sent to Furly and to others to criticise, probably represented Penn's own view. We should expect him to begin, as this frame does, with the provision for religious liberty. It was the cause which he had nearest at heart, and the commercial and practical arguments with which it is supported are ones that he had been fond of using in the controversy on toleration in England. The allusion to Venice as the precedent for the ballot can be paralleled from his " Plan for the Union of Europe," and the fundamental nature of Magna Carta was a very favourite theme of his.

The preamble is an interesting composition. Beginning with moralisings on the fall of man and the consequent need of law, it proceeds to lay stress on the identity of interest between governor and governed and the subservience of government to " the general good," and concludes with remarks on the responsibility attached to the founders of constitutions, bidding them give a careful study to the Jewish and the English systems and recognise the general value of an understanding of comparative politics, so that they can borrow whatever conduces to " the end of government, to wit, the virtue, peace and Prosperity of the People, to which all forms and customs ought to yield." In certain respects the frame itself differs from the one finally adopted. The Assembly has the right of proposing legislation, and is to consist of as many as 384, elected after a division of the country into 24 counties, 96 hundreds, and 192 tribes. The composition of the Council and its committees is much the same. But the governor has the additional power of fourteen days' suspensory veto. The equal division of property among the children is qualified by the Jewish exception that the eldest son should have a double share. Otherwise there is the same democratic, benevolent, and paternal spirit as that which characterises the final scheme.

The aristocratic one, which was sent to T. R. and others, probably represented the desires of the more important adventurers, who had bought land in the new colony. The scheme provided for a hereditary landed Upper House not unlike that of Carolina. A " baronage " of 5000 acres was to give a seat, which was to be forfeited if the baronage fell below 2000 acres. The Lower House was to be composed of delegates elected every year—one for every 20,000 acres of the land. In addition to these houses, there was to be a council chosen from members of the two chambers and organised into committees to assist the governor in administration of affairs. Land was to be made the title to office, and there was to be a hereditary chamber, which would ill agree with the principle of the equal division of property among the children.

The great difference between the democratic and the aristocratic scheme lay in the composition of the Upper House. Round this there was apparently a great struggle. The correspondent signing himself with the initials T. R. took great exception to the idea of making land the sole title to a seat. He considered

the proposal an unintelligent imitation of the House of
Lords, quite unsuitable for a new country. He was
himself opposed to the principle of government by two
chambers. He thought collisions inevitable, and
wished boldly to cut the knot by having only one
chamber, as in all the other colonies and in the early
days of England herself. We cannot tell how much
these arguments influenced Penn ; but at all events
the landed house was abandoned, and the superfluity
of bodies created by the existence of a council and
two chambers was modified.

It was agreed that the Upper House should be an
elective body, composed of men " noted for their
virtue, wisdom and ability " or " substance." Of
course " substance " in Pennsylvania could mean
nothing but " land " ; but it was merely hinted at as
a suitable qualification and not as the sole title to
office. It was much more difficult to determine the
functions of this body than its composition. We can
see from the variations and erasures in the different
drafts the trouble that it caused. There were many
things to be considered. It was necessary to com-
pensate the expectant landowners, who were disappointed in the composition of the Upper House ; the
democratic basis of the government had still to be
kept ; but it was necessary also to prevent the democracy from running uncontrolled. So it was settled
that there should be two bodies : the first composed of
men of wealth and eminence, with the duty of proposing matters for legislation ; the second composed
of less distinguished men, with the duty of deciding on
their proposals.

The reasons for choosing this solution were various.
In the first place, the danger of deadlocks was minimised without resorting to the system of three chambers

proposed by some of Penn's advisers, and without adopting the remaining alternative of single-chamber government. In the second place, it was a concession to the aristocratic ideal, and at the same time an extension of the constitutional referendum. This is shown in the words of one of the earlier drafts formed before it was decided to have this representative body : " that all laws prepared by the Great Council or Senate may have the more full countenance of the inhabitants of the province, according to the words of the patent, and so more obligatory upon them, it is agreed that during the infancy of the said province, that the present inhabitants shall at all times upon notice given them by the Great Council or Senate, and after conferring with themselves they shall give their negative or affirmative, which to them seemeth best." In the third place, it was a simple plan that had also the theoretical merit of keeping the executive (which was largely in the hands of the Upper House) separate from the legislative.

When the Upper House had once been constituted, it was apparently easy to settle the other points. For though Furly criticised the long terms of office (he wanted their duration to be measured by months and not years) and the method of appointing officers, which had been taken from his own country, there were certain things that were taken for granted and appeared in almost all the drafts.

The principle of the ballot was accepted, whether it was to be based on the precedent of Venice or " the Royal Society at Gresham College." All elections were to be made by its help. The only source of dispute was the extent of its use in Parliament ; for some wanted to employ it always, others only in " questions relating to personal matters." And it was considered desirable to have the written votes of members where it was possible. Rotation was also accepted, and the only question was whether the Upper House should consist of two or of three series. The restriction of the governor's power was equally unquestioned, and it had only to be settled whether the governor should have two or three votes in the Upper House. With regard to the committees, the only point to decide was their number and their duties. The fundamental nature of the constitution, and nearly all the other provisions, met with no opposition ; and so the final draft was signed and accepted.

This sketch of the birth of the constitution serves to show that it was not, as might appear from reading the document alone, the work of a single student of Harrington. But none the less it appears that his writings were the inspiration of the ideas.

In the first place, the unpublished drafts bear marks of his influence which supplement the evidence of the constitution itself. Bamfield's scheme contains a proposal for making marriage a qualification for Parliament—a suggestion that occurs in " Oceana." [1] It also lays down the correct age for the marriage of men and women and their duties to their poorer relatives—a suggestion that savours of Utopias. Another of the schemes proposes the institution of twelve leading citizens as conservators of the Charter, with the duty of declaring void all measures that contravene the constitution—an idea that was favoured by Harrington as well as a few of his contemporaries. The words " propose " " resolve," occur. And a division of the country similar to that suggested in " Oceana " was proposed. The rejected house of proprietors was directly built up on the theory of the balance of pro-

[1] *Cf.* the similar qualification for the Anciens in the Constitution of the year III.

perty : for, unlike our House of Lords, loss of property carried with it loss of membership.

In the second place, in the preamble to the accepted form of the constitution there are unmistakable allusions to Harrington's writings. Whether the writing of a theoretical preamble in this, as in other colonial constitutions of the Restoration period, was due to Harrington's influence or not cannot be maintained with certainty. At any rate the custom started in this period, and it may very well have been suggested by " Oceana," where the description of the constitution is preceded by an academic section showing the theory of government on which it is based. In his preamble Penn, like Harrington, abandoned the old classification of governments. " I know," he wrote, " what is said by the several admirers of *monarchy*, *aristocracy* and *democracy*, which are the rule of one, a few, and many, and are the three common ideas of government, when men discourse on the subject. But I choose to solve the controversy with this small distinction, and it belongs to all three : *Any government is free to the people under it* (whatever be the frame) *where the laws rule and the people are a party to those laws*, and more than this is tyranny, oligarchy or confusion." Unlike him, he refused to believe in the theory of the perpetuity of good governments. He referred to the theory only to reject it. " Governments, like clocks, go from the motion men give them ; and, as governments are made and moved by men, so by them they are ruined too. . . . If men be bad, let the government be never so good, they will endeavour to warp it and spoil it to their turn." " I know," he continued, " some say, let us have good laws, and no matter for the men that execute them : but let them consider that though good laws do well, good men do better : for good laws may want good men, and be abolished or evaded by ill men ; but good men will never want good laws, nor suffer ill ones." All these remarks seem to be directed against Harrington and his school, but the conclusion that the object of government is " To support power in reverence with the people, and to secure the people from the abuse of power," is the epitome of all Harrington's philosophy.

In the third place it should be noticed that the three provisions of the Constitution which Penn himself seems to have cherished most are the three things to which the greatest prominence was given in " Oceana " —the ballot, rotation, and the separation of the functions of debate and result. All these three things he defended in language that reminds one very much of Harrington.

At one time he spoke of his " dislike at their disliking the model of an elected Council to prepare an Assembly to resolve, and at throwing away the use of the Ballot, which their children, as I told them, will have, perhaps, cause sufficient to repent of their folly therein."[1] At another time he wrote thus of the assembly : " If they turn debaters or judges or complainers, you overthrow the charter quite in the very root of the constitution of it, for that is to usurp the provincial council's part in the charter, and to forfeit the charter itself ; here would be two assemblies and two representatives, whereas they are but one to two works, one prepares and proposes, the other assents or denies. The negative voice is by that in them, and that is not a debating, mending, altering, but an accepting power."[2] On another occasion he spoke to much the same purpose. " The ablest men have always been chosen to be of the

[1] Penn and Logan," Correspondence," ii. 18.
[2] Hazard, " Register," iv. 105.

Council to prepare the laws, and the Assembly are to consent to them. Though two bodies, yet are we but one power—the one prepares, the other consents." [1]

His belief in rotation was equally strong. " There is," he wrote, " an excess of vanity that is apt to creep in upon the people in power in America, who, having got out of the crowd in which they were lost here, upon every little eminency there think nothing taller than themselves but the trees, and as if there were no after superior judgment to which they should be accountable ; so that I have sometimes thought that, if there was a law to oblige the people in power in their respective colonies to take turns in coming over for England, that they might lose themselves again amongst the crowds of so much more considerable people at the custom house, exchange, and Westminster Hall, they would exceedingly amend in their conduct at their return, and be much more discreet and tractable, and fit for government." [2]

Finally the greatest of all Pennsylvanians, Benjamin Franklin, was of opinion that the first constitution of the colony " savoured very strongly of Harrington and his Oceana." [3] Unfortunately Penn's library cannot now be traced ; so it is impossible to say whether Penn himself possessed a copy of " Oceana." It is, however, interesting to know that James Logan, Penn's trusted secretary of state, a man who tried to carry out Penn's ideas and was for that reason accused of following " the pernicious rules " of " beloved Machiavel " and other " high-flown statesmen," possessed a first edition of the book. On his death in 1752 his books were set aside to form the foundation for the " Library Company

[1] Janney, " Life of Penn," p. 410.

[2] Shepherd, " Pennsylvania as a proprietary colony," p. 311.

[3] " Historical Review of the Constitution and Government of Pennsylvania," p. 13.

of Philadelphia." In addition to one copy of Toland's edition, this first of American public libraries had three first editions of " Oceana," which, if they did not all belong to Logan himself, belonged to members of his family or early colonists. Too much importance should not be placed in this fact, but it is not irrelevant in trying to determine the influence of Harrington on the Pennsylvanian constitution.

There is no evidence, which is absolutely conclusive, that " Oceana " was consulted ; but with all these considerations, with the *à priori* grounds, with the parallel influence in Carolina and the Jerseys before us, it must be considered a moral certainty. It would indeed be a very striking coincidence if Penn chose from the Continent just the things that Harrington had chosen before him, and one that is worthy of record. The whole question may be called puny, but the practical influence of political writings is a subject of some interest to the historian, and any fresh example is valuable. Penn might very well have got his ideas direct from the Continent, but the evidence seems to show that he got them mainly through " Oceana," just as the framers of the Constitution of the Australian Commonwealth appear to have got many of their ideas on federalism, including the title of their new federation, from Bryce's " American Commonwealth." [1]

Whatever its origin may have been, the constitution was an utter failure, and the things that disappeared were the things that were taken from " Oceana." Alterations began at once, and the soundness of Sidney's and Furly's belief in the necessity for making provision for alterations was quickly seen. The very first entry in the journal of the Council was the proposal to repeal the law for

---

[1] *Cf.* W. H. Moore, " The Australian Commonwealth," p. 66.

the general use of the ballot and to confine it, as had
been proposed earlier, to questions of a personal
nature. By 1689 they had gone further. The ballot
had been generally given up in elections. Beans
or tickets were used in some of the counties, but the
general opinion seems to have been that the ballot
was never meant to be the normal procedure. In
the words of one of the speakers in the debate which
arose round the question, " the use of the ballot is
where there is a doubt." [1]   That is to say, if a show
of hands or acclamation cannot satisfactorily show
the people's choice, the ballot has to be resorted to ;
otherwise it is unnecessary. And so the people gave
it up. " They valued themselves," wrote Oldmixon,
" and with good reason in the main, on being *Englishmen*, and scorn'd, as they said, to give their opinions
in the dark ; they would do nothing which they
durst not own, and their foreheads and their voices
should always agree with one another. Thus they
clamoured against that part of the constitution which
secur'd the rest, the election by ballot, and never
gave over clamouring till it was abolished, and the
first order of government broken in upon in the most
essential parts of it." [2]

A second cause of dispute was the size of the
Parliament. It will be remembered that the constitution provided for a council of 72 and an assembly
of 200. T. R. had told Penn that the numbers were
too great, but his opinion had apparently not been
shared by all ; for it was suggested that the assembly
should consist of as many as 1000. The people were
of T. R.'s opinion. They argued that with the land
to be occupied it was impossible for so many to give

<hr>

[1] Colonial Records of Pennsylvania, i. 279-83.
[2] Oldmixon, " The British Empire in America," pp. 170-71.

up their time to attending the assembly. Theoretically Harrington's aphorism — " The Popular Assembly in a Commonwealth may consist of too few but can never consist of too many "[1]—may have been right, but practical considerations were too strong. The people won their point, and in the first year of the corporate existence of the colony the numbers of the Council and Assembly were reduced to 18 and 36 respectively.

The most important struggle of all centred round the powers of the assembly. It is a characteristic of human nature that when a number of men are gathered together they will talk, particularly if all those men are interested in politics. It was all very well for Penn to continue to say, " They have an I or a no . . . but not a Debating power." It was his theory, as it was Harrington's theory, but it did not work. It cannot be said that the idea was undemocratic. It was not like Maryland, where the governor had continually tried to reserve the right of initiating measures with the Council which he himself appointed. It was not like Carolina, where the Council was composed of hereditary landowners with life membership. Penn tried to point this out. He told them that the Council was an elective body, which corresponded to the Commons and not the Lords, and he called it a " false notion " to hold that this elective body was not the people's representative. He argued in vain, for he was arguing on entirely different lines from his opponents.

Penn took the theoretical standpoint. Holding government to be " an expedient against confusion," he was afraid that confusion would arise if two bodies were given similar powers. So he gave one house

[1] " Political Aphorisms," p. 519.

the right to initiate, the other house the veto power. To give to the assembly the right to propose legislation and the consequent right " to meet at all times during the year, without the Governor's concurrence," would be " to distort government, to break the due proportion of the parts of it, and to make the legislative the executive part of it." [1] So he stuck to Harrington's theory, which was in reality perfectly democratic.

But no theoretical grounds would weigh with the assembly. Penn protested in vain. As an assembly they claimed the rights of all other assemblies, and in 1701 they eventually got what they wanted and the Council ceased to be a legislative body.

In this way almost all the provisions that seem to have been borrowed from " Oceana " were thrown over, and the last attempt to introduce Harrington's ideas in an American colony met with utter failure. Such is so often the fate of plans that are based primarily on theory.

The civil and religious liberty which were to be secured by all these theoretical devices remained when the devices disappeared. Pennsylvania immediately achieved European fame. Voltaire and Montesquieu wrote of it in terms of great admiration. Coleridge and Wordsworth talked of emigrating to it. Its success influenced the movement for greater freedom of religion in New England. Pennsylvanians streamed through the Cumberland Valley and along the National Post Road to occupy the territory that afterwards became the States of Kentucky, Ohio, and Indiana. They took with them a belief in democracy, toleration, and small holdings. They had abandoned many of the more peculiar things that Penn and Harrington alike had stood for : but

---

[1] Proud, " Pennsylvania," ii. 48-49.

they had accepted the great things, the principles
of democracy and toleration.

When Pennsylvania became a State many of
these rejected ideas were again established. It took
four years, and the moral pressure of all the other
States for the double chamber system to be re-adopted.
But the ballot returned at once and along with it,
(so as to avoid an "inconvenient aristocracy")
rotation in the executive Council.

Penn's idea that government could not be for the
interests of one man came back; and the Council
of Censors, which had appeared in one of the draft
frames, reappeared with the provision for the public
posting of bills.

The attempts to introduce Harrington's ideas
into the colonies of the Restoration period were on
the whole failures. But it is probable that his influence was still felt. The belief in property qualifications which held sway so long in America must
have been supported by the scientific basis which
he gave to the power of the landowner. The definite
conception of civil and religious liberty must be
attributed in part to his theories. And the American
belief in the sanctity of written constitutions must
have been partly inspired by his faith in the rule of
laws, and his cherished opinion that if only institutions are sufficiently good they stand in no need of
change. The next chapter will show that even the
more concrete things for which he stood were many
of them adopted at the time of the Revolution after
having been rejected in the previous century.

There can be little doubt that, if Harrington's
mind had remained sound, he would himself have
been invited to produce a constitution for some

infant colony, and would have established Oceana in America. In those circumstances his influence on the colonies of the seventeenth century would have been greater still. But even now though less direct it was not insignificant. As predecessor on the one hand of the Whigs, who administered the colonies from the Council of Trade, and on the other hand of the republicans, who made their constitutions, he was a vital force in America. And it is not without reason that his writings have been more admired and read on the other side of the Atlantic than in England.

CHAPTER VIII

HARRINGTON'S INFLUENCE ON THE AMERICAN REVOLUTION

§ I

THE second of the two periods at which the influence of Harrington was felt in America was the age of the revolution.

The American Revolution, like all revolutions, may be divided into two parts—the first the period of destruction, when the old was being broken, the second the period of construction, when the new was being built. All that was done away with was the authority of the English King and Parliament. The rest of the structure, which had been steadily built up for more than a century, was kept, elaborated, and completed. The two periods inevitably over-lapped one another, as, even after the separation had been achieved, it was necessary to keep on repeating its justification. But the Declaration of Independence can be taken roughly as the dividing point.

During the period of destruction the writer to whom the Americans turned with the greatest faith and frequency was Locke. His writings were already classics. Many of his opinions were accepted in England. He was an eminently respectable authority, who could not be called "seditious" or "levelling," for he was a Churchman, and his books had been written to justify the monarchy of William III.[1] But still with admirable simplicity and emphasis

[1] *Cf.* Otis, " A vindication of the conduct of the House of Representatives of the Province of Massachusetts Bay," pp. 19 and 20, 1762.

he had given expression to the sanctity of liberty
and property and the theory that government rests
on consent. He was consequently quoted in pamphlets, newspapers, sermons, town meetings. His
books were advertised for sale in the papers. Where-
ever politics were talked about or written about,
the name of Locke was magic. It was found that
he justified what America, largely for commercial
and economic reasons, wanted. His influence was
not merely an academic influence, and his works
did not merely provide material for happy quota-
tions. He actually helped to form the ideas of the
people and make them conscious revolutionaries in
possession of theories.

There were many other writers besides Locke
who were studied and quoted; for the men who
had most to do with the separation from England,
were for the most part great readers. John Adams,
who seems to have written almost consciously for a
posterity that never reads him, gives two or three
lists of the writers who were most read in his day
and in his judgment influenced American opinion
most. They belonged to three periods of English
history, the Reformation, the Interregnum, the Revolution of 1688. In the first came translations
and criticisms of Machiavelli; in the second, Harrington, Milton, and the " Vindiciæ contra Tyrannos ";
in the third, Sidney, Locke, Hoadley, Trenchard,
Gordon, " Plato Redivivus." These are names that
all occur with more or less frequency in the fugitive
literature of the day.

Their influence was of three kinds. They were
read to find theories and justifications of revolution. Their authority was quoted academically to
give weight to an argument already found. Their

examples were kept before the public eye to encourage an enthusiasm for liberty.

The theory of revolution which John Adams derived from Harrington was interesting and ingenious. It appeared in the articles which he wrote to the "Boston Gazette" in 1774, under the signature of Novanglus. In the first place he took the line which Turgot took, that colonies must sooner or later fall away from the mother country. In other words he justified colonial independence as a natural law, and quoted Harrington's account of Roman colonisation to bear this out.[1] Then, citing Harrington's famous prophecy of American independence, he proceeded to particularise on British colonies.[2] His argument here was that America must be independent and no part of the British Empire, for the simple reason that the British Empire does not exist. Great Britain is in reality one of Harrington's republics, "a government of laws and not of men" —with the King its first magistrate.[3] There is no such thing as a colony to English Common Law. The plantations were actually given legislative sovereignty in their charters. And the land does not even belong to the King or the Parliament to justify their dominion. And so from every point of view the attitude of George III. and his counsellors was indefensible. Much of Adams' contention

---

[1] Adams, "Works," iv. 103. "The commonwealth of Rome, by planting colonies of its citizens, within the bounds of Italy, took the best way of propagating itself and naturalising the country ; whereas if it had planted such colonies without the bounds of Italy, it would have alienated the citizens and given root to liberty abroad, that might have sprung up foreign or savage and hostile to her."

[2] Cf. above, p. 67.
As early as 1711 Harrington's prophecy had been noticed as " a Reflexion that deserves some consideration," by Robert Hunter, Governor of New York.

[3] Cf. Mably's theory of monarchical republics.

was sound, and the idea of the natural independence
of colonies was one that would have weight with
the theorising type of mind.

An instance of the citation of Harrington's name
to lend weight to an accepted theory may be taken
from these same articles of Adams. The writer has
been speaking of the equality of man, the sovereignty
of the people, their delegation of power to the King,
and their right to resume it. He suddenly breaks
off. "These are what are called revolution principles. They are the principles of Aristotle and
Plato, of Livy and Cicero, and Sidney, Harrington,
and Locke; the principles of nature and eternal
reason; the principle on which the whole government over us now stands."[1] Appeals, like this,
to the names of writers and statesmen of unchallenged
repute were not uncommon.

The names of the great apostles and martyrs of
liberty have always been used with good effect for
the purpose of inspiring the people. The words
Harmodius and Aristogeiton sent a thrill through
the ordinary Greek mind. A reference to the Barons
at Runnymede braced the quieter English imagination. The names Brutus and Cassius intoxicated
the French people. In America, where the cult of
Liberty flourished as it never flourished anywhere
outside Paris, the same thing is true. Hampden
was the great, wise, independent citizen, the Cato
of the English-speaking race. Algernon Sidney was
the high-souled martyr who gave his life for the
cause of freedom; people called their children with
his name.[2] Harrington, who went mad in the same

---

[1] Adams, "Works," iv. 15.

[2] In France, too, he was quoted alongside of the heroes of the Roman
Republic (Aulard, "French Revolution," I. iii.).

cause, was the man who used the powers of his mind, his knowledge and his reason for liberty. In the oration which was delivered over the body of General Joseph Warren, the hero and martyr of the battle of Bunkers Hill, the panegyrist broke forth into these words: " Like Harrington he wrote—like Cicero he spoke—like Hampden he lived—and like Wolfe he died." [1] The speech in which this passage occurs was long famous in America.

In three respects Harrington played his part in the destructive part of the American Revolution. As prophet of independence, as exponent of popular sovereignty, as apostle of liberty he was set before the American people. He was not so widely referred to as Locke, Sidney, Hampden and a few others. But he was one of the theorists whose books helped to separate America from England. James Otis and John Adams, whose writings led the early attack on the English Parliament, were both fervent admirers, who spoke in no doubtful terms of his greatness.

§ 2

With the constructive part of the revolution the name of Locke gave way to that of Montesquieu. Locke and Sidney and others were still quoted. But whenever an argument was to be clinched it was now Montesquieu, and if not Montesquieu, Blackstone, whose opinions were summoned. America had determined that if she had broken away from England she was still going to hold by English political institutions. So she turned with a great seriousness to the great exponents and critics of the English Constitution. With their help she hoped to

[1] Loring, " Hundred Boston Orators," p. 129.

be able to forge a new link to the chain, which had started from Magna Carta and had been continued through Confirmatio Cartarum, the Petition of Right, and the Bill of Rights.

This fact alone serves to show the sanity of the American revolutionaries. They were great readers and highly educated men, but still they did not become doctrinaires. No Socialists sprang up.[1] There was nothing like the Diggers' outbreak and the other curious features of the Puritan rebellion. No Utopias were written. Not even an Abbé Sieyès arose. Ferment there was, but the people remained sane. They were, most of them, farmers in close contact with the pure wholesome earth. They were not unused to self-government and liberty. And they knew exactly what they wanted. The framers of the constitution thought not of a new heaven and a new earth. They set to work solemnly and practically to establish on a different footing the institutions which had already been enjoyed in colonial times and incorporated in charters, frames of government, and laws, and to carry on the ideas of freedom and good sense with which the name of England was associated.

Had there been a religious upheaval at the same time, there is little doubt that the American Revolution would have been a different story. But England had not touched the religious freedom of her colonies, nor had the influence of Voltaire and Rousseau travelled across the Atlantic. The Americans were still mostly staunch Puritans, with their religion unattacked and their beliefs unchallenged.

For these reasons one might expect that a book possessing the fantastic features which mark

---

[1] Except some Pennsylvanians, who clamoured for an " agrarian."

" Oceana " would be passed over. And there seems little doubt that these features told against it. But nevertheless the book was read. For it was what the Americans wanted, a criticism of English institutions. Furthermore, it belonged to the Puritan era of English literature.

It is very difficult to state the direct influence of the book during the formation of the State constitutions. It is tempting, for instance, to see allusions to Harrington in the Virginia Bill of Rights, the model of all the other Bills.[1] But evidence is wanting, and we cannot tread on certain ground till we come to John Adams.

The second President of the United States stands very high in the ranks of the great men who arose to guide the American Colonies through their great crisis. Unlike most of them, he played a prominent part both in the destructive and constructive periods. He was not a member of the body which formed the federal Constitution, being engaged at the time in diplomatic work in Europe. But he had great influence in the formation of the Constitutions of Virginia, Pennsylvania, New York, and Carolina, in addition to that of his own native Massachusetts. Himself a perfect English gentleman, he had a firm belief in the existence of a natural aristocracy. Like Harrington, he believed in republicanism rather than democracy. As long as a government was one of laws and not of men, and as long as it was one " in

---

[1] Section 5 runs as follows : " That the legislative and executive powers of the State should be separate and distinct from the judiciary ; and that the members of the two first may be restrained from oppression by feeling and participating the burdens of the people, they should at fixed periods, be reduced to a private station, return into that body from which they were originally taken, and the vacancies be supplied by frequent, certain, and regular elections, in which, all or any part of the former members, to be again eligible or ineligible, as the laws shall direct."

which the people have collectively, or by representation, an essential share in the sovereignty," Adams was satisfied.[1] " A simple and perfect democracy never yet existed among men." All through his political career he stood for the system of checks and balances, for which America had become famous. He possessed two copies of Harrington's works, which are now in the Boston Public Library. He remarked in 1812 that he had read them forty or fifty years ago. And the most hurried perusal of his writings shows to what good purpose he had done so.

In the year 1776, while the transition from royal to republican government was worrying many minds, Adams wrote his " Thoughts on Government applicable to the Present State of the American Colonies." It was written as a private letter to a friend in Virginia, but it was published in Philadelphia. Richard Henry Lee and Patrick Henry were both interested readers ; and an almost exact replica was sent on application from the delegates of North Carolina and New Jersey, who had assembled to produce constitutions for their States. In this way the political ideas which Adams held in 1776 were widely diffused, and were of great importance in the history of the State constitutions.

The letter struck the American note at once. It asked for an " empire of laws," which could only be achieved by a division of the legislature into two houses, by the separation of the three functions of government, and by rotation. It insisted on the elective principle, and suggested indirect election for the Upper House. The name of Harrington was mentioned in the letter along with other names.

---

[1] This was Montesquieu's definition of a republic.

Like the other States Massachusetts also embarked upon the task of forming a constitution. The first attempt failed, and in 1778 the towns to which the proposed constitution was referred rejected it.   But it was obvious that the temporary government, under which the State then was, could not be final.   Iu September 1779 a Convention was called, which " resolved unanimously that the government to be framed by this convention shall be a FREE REPUBLIC," and " resolved that it is of the essence of a free republic, that the people be governed by FIXED LAWS OF THEIR OWN MAKING." [1] The task of designing the frame was entrusted to Adams, whose proposals were accepted with almost no alteration and finally approved by the town meetings of Massachusetts.   Such was the success of the constitution that it exists in all its essential features to this day.   Its fame is only equalled by the constitution made for the State of New York by John Jay.

In this constitution Adams formulated the scheme which he had already suggested for Virginia, N. Carolina, and New Jersey.   He no longer proposed the indirect election of the Upper House, but otherwise he stood firm by his belief in checks and balances, and he introduced, as had been done in other States, a property qualification for voters and candidates.   The last words of the Bill of Rights, which were as emphatic as the parallel passage in the Virginian Bill was comprehensive, were attributed in the debates on the revision of the Constitution in 1853 to the direct influence of Harrington,[2] and a recent writer has expressed the same opinion.[3]   The passage runs as

---

[1] Adams, " Works," iv. 215.   [2] Debates of the Convention, p. 120.
[3] Theodore Dwight, " Political Science Quarterly," March 1887

follows : " In the government of this commonwealth, the legislative department shall never exercise the executive and judicial powers or either of them ; the executive shall never exercise the legislative and judicial powers or either of them ; the judicial shall never exercise the legislative powers, or either of them ; to the end it may be a government of laws and not of men." It need not be supposed that all those who spoke of " the government of laws and not of men " were consciously quoting Harrington, but we know that Adams himself attributed the English translation of this classical phrase to him.[1] Other phrases and features of the constitution may perhaps be referred to the same source ; but guesswork is unprofitable. It is more important to emphasise the one certain fact that we have.

The opening words of the Frame of Government run as follows : " The people inhabiting the territory heretofore [formerly] called the Province of Massachusetts Bay, do hereby solemnly and mutually agree with each other to form themselves into a free sovereign, and independent body politic, or State, by the Name of the Commonwealth of Massachusetts." During the discussion of this in the Convention we read that " on a motion made and seconded, that the word ' Massachusetts ' be expunged, and that the word ' Oceana ' be substituted, the same was put and passed in the negative." [2]

We just read the bare entry in the Journal of the Convention and we hear no more about it. It may have been a satirical proposal accusing Adams of plagiarism, or it may have been a serious suggestion by some Harringtonian enthusiast, to whom the word Oceana naturally followed the word Common-

---

[1] *Cf.* John Adams " Works," iv. 106.   [2] " Journal of the Convention," p. 43.

wealth. In the old days as colony, as province, and even as state, the title Massachusetts Bay had been used. But in the constitution which was now being proposed the word Bay was to be dropped and the title of Commonwealth was to be assumed. As this slight alteration was to be made it is quite intelligible that a larger alteration should be thought desirable. The only other State that had an Indian name was Connecticut. Oceana was a not unsuitable name for a maritime state, whose citizens gained their livelihood largely from the sea. And it was a name that would show to the world the efforts which had been made by the authors of the constitution to establish the most perfect republican government they could.

But, whether satirical or serious, the proposal seems to show that people connected Adams' political ideas with Harrington and saw the influence of Oceana in the proposed constitution.

We can hardly say that there was a cult of Harrington in New England, but his name was held in peculiar veneration. James Otis, the first of the Massachusetts revolutionaries, spoke of " the great, the incomparable Harrington " and " his Oceana and other divine writings." [1] Dr Stiles, in a sermon preached at Hartford in 1783 in order to eulogise New England, declared that she had " realised the capital ideas of Oceana." [3] John Adams was one of the most fervent devotees that Harrington ever had. We find his son, when President of the United States, turning to Harrington to look up some political point.[3] H. G. Otis, mayor of Boston in 1830, appeals to the memory of " the Lockes and

---

[1] " Rights of the British Colonies," 2nd edition, p. 10.
[2] J. W. Thornton, " Pulpit of the American Revolution," p. 404.
[3] J. Q. Adams, " Works," ix. 228.

Sidneys and Miltons and Harringtons." [1]   In 1853
Rufus Choate, one of the leading lawyers and citizens
of the day, in allusion to Harrington, besought his
fellow members to spare the " historical phrases of the
old glorious school of liberty . . . as they would spare
the general English of the Bible." [2]   And the number
of copies of Harrington's works which have found
their way into the Boston Public Library and Boston
Athenæum is a further evidence of his popularity.[3]

But we must return to our discussion of Adams.
His work was not finished when he had planned
the government of his native state, but he was called
upon to leave the immediate scene of action in order
to represent his country in European diplomacy.
He found both in England and France a lively interest being taken in the experimental State Constitutions.   The   merits   of   the   Constitutions   of
Pennsylvania and Massachusetts were respectively
canvassed by supporters of single- and double-chamber
government.   To facilitate discussion and to arouse
greater interest French translations were made of
their frames of government.   The old battle began
again, and the arguments that had been used by
Milton and Nedham or the supporters of the Long
Parliament against Harrington or the Cromwellians
were again repeated.   Dr Price, whose pamphlets
met with a wonderful popularity, was backed up by
Turgot and Mirabeau in his eulogies of the concentration of power.   Not only was double-chamber
government laughed at, but the whole system of
checks and balances and the idea of the government
of laws was attacked with biting criticism.

---

[1] Colonial Society. of Massachusetts "Publications," v. 288
[2] Massachusetts Convention Debates, p. 120.
[3] A copy of " Oceana " was in the library of Harvard as early as 1723.

The attack made little impression in America. Even Pennsylvania resorted to double - chamber government after four years. But Adams not unnaturally regarded European criticism as partially personal, for he took pride in the part that he himself had played in forming the State Constitutions. He therefore determined to take up his cudgels in their defence. The work which he produced was as monumental as it was disorderly, consisting of a review of the systems of government in Europe since classical times and an account of the great political writers, philosophers, and historians as far as they threw any light on the theory of checks and balances.[1]

The first part of the " Defence of the Constitutions of the United States " was published in 1787 and transmitted immediately to America. It was read by the delegates assembled at Philadelphia to form the Federal Constitution, and it may have confirmed some in their allegiance to the system of checks and balances. But in the present connection it is important not so much for the influence which it may have exercised as for the additional light which it throws on the history of Adams' political ideas. Adams himself claimed that it also threw light on the political ideas of other American statesmen of the time. " As the writer was personally acquainted with most of the gentlemen in each of the States, who had the principal share in the first drafts," he wrote in the preface, " the following work was really written to lay before the public a specimen of that kind of reading and reasoning which produced the

---

[1] The treatment is historical, and systems of government and writers are marshalled in much the same way as they were marshalled by Harrington to prove the theory of the balance of property, and the value of separating debate and result.

American constitutions." [1] As far as the gentlemen
to whom he refers are concerned, it is probable that
Harrington's influence is exaggerated and the space
which is allotted to him among the political writers
is unduly liberal. But of Adams' own debt to Harrington there can be no doubt, and the " Defence "
affords fresh proof. The point, which was really
at the root of Adams' advocacy of double-chamber
government was Harrington's conception of the
" natural aristocracy " which exists in all communi-
ties. His argument was this. These natural aristocrats, being born leaders, would at once become
tyrants, if benevolent tryants, under a single-chamber
system. The only way to avoid this contradiction
of the republican principle of the " government of
laws " is to give them a chamber to themselves, where
they will serve as a check to the more popular house.[2]
" The great art of lawgiving," he wrote later, " consists in balancing the poor against the rich in the
legislature." [3] Adams was enough of a democrat
to believe in the sovereignty of the people ; and he
felt that this was secured by the balance of property
in America, nineteen-twentieths of the land being
in possession of the people.[4] But he was determined
to save his country from the extreme form of democracy. Double-chamber government seemed to him
one of the most useful safeguards against it, and in
advocating it he made an effective use of the arguments which Harrington had employed for his own
peculiar double-chamber system. In short, we
gather from this book that it was from Harrington

[1] Adams, " Works," iv. 293.
[2] *Ibid.* iv. 404 and 410-12. Besides Harrington's description of the
natural aristocracy and the government of laws he quotes the passage about
the two girls and the cake. See above, p. 51.
[3] *Ibid.* vi. 280.   [4] *Ibid.* iv. 359.

that Adams drew the conservative ideas, by which
he exercised most influence in his country—his belief
in the rule of law, his belief in the natural aristocracy,
and his belief in the whole system of checks and
balances.

It is possible now to sum up the influence of Harrington in America. As one of the small band of
liberal and republican authors, whom the Americans
studied, he helped to produce the atmosphere of
republicanism, in which independence was declared.
His influence on American institutions is, however,
also definite. The final adoption of the ballot is
largely due to the colonial precedents of Carolina,
Pennsylvania, and New Jersey where the electoral
methods suggested for " Oceana " were imitated.
Rotation in the Senate was taken from Franklin's
Articles of Confederation and borrowed by him from
these same middle colonies. The eventual predominance of the double-chamber system must be attributed
largely to Adams—whose debt to Harrington has
been indicated. The confidence felt in written constitutions was inspired by the doctrinaire belief in
an empire of laws, and the lasting nature with which
the author of " Oceana " credited them. Finally
it was Harrington who had formed a theory which
could make John Dickinson write that " a landed
interest widely diffused, by the personal virtues of
honest industry, fair dealing and laudable frugality,
is the firmest foundation that can be laid for the
secure establishment of civil liberty and national
independence,"[1] which could make Noah Webster

[1] The passage which precedes this shows clearly the influence, conscious or
unconscious, of Harrington. " By the policy of Henry the Seventh of England,
in order to strengthen himself against the nobility, the acquisition of property
in lands by the Commons was facilitated."

argue that " A general and tolerably equal distribution of landed property is the whole basis of national
freedom.   The system of the great Montesquieu will
ever be erroneous, till the words property or lands
in fee-simple are substituted for virtue throughout
the Spirit of Laws,"[1] which could make Jefferson
call the abolition of primogeniture " the best of all
Agrarian laws," placing this and the abolition of
entails alongside of religious liberty and popular
education as the four great preservatives of liberty
and democracy.[2] Washington believed in the agri-
cultural republic from a moral point of view, Franklin
from an economic point of view ; these men added
the political point of view.

[1] Webster is basing this passage on Moyle, who has been referred to above
as almost a plagiarist of Harrington.

[2] Jefferson's copy of " Oceana " is still to be seen in the Library of Congress
at Washington.

CHAPTER IX

THE part played by theorists in bringing on the French Revolution has been and will be a matter for difference of opinion. Their influence in the political reconstruction is evident to all.

It is impossible here to enter into a detailed discussion of this, but certain facts may be noticed. The classics played a far more important part than they ever played in the English Rebellion. They were quoted not only to stimulate a love of liberty, but also to engender a belief in the power of legislation. Lycurgus, popularised by Plutarch, might any day be reincarnated and make a constitution for France. And names, proposed or adopted, such as consuls, tribunes, censors, ephors, areopagites, as well as councils and senates, were constant reminders of the revival of the Greek and Roman ideals. The English Rebellion with its Hampden, its Sidney, and its Cromwell was studied with a certain amount of interest ; its literature was translated ; its causes and its failure were discussed ; and its constitutional experiments were recalled. The American Revolution, in which so many Frenchmen had themselves been engaged, was observed in all its phases. Its constructive side especially was followed with critical eyes. The State constitutions were translated and discussed in pamphlets. Adams' defence of them appeared in a French edition. The Federal Constitution was read by everybody. American nomenclature was borrowed for Bills of Rights, National

Conventions, and Committees of Public Safety.   The whole history of a revolution that had taken place so recently attracted the liveliest attention.   It was, in fact, taken for granted that all educated Frenchmen had studied the classics and knew all that could at that time be known of the English and American Revolutions.

How far Harrington had been read in France during the eighteenth century is not easy to determine.   Bernard had published extracts and summaries of his works in French in the two literary periodicals which he was editing in the Netherlands.[1]   And one can well imagine that the Economists with their belief in the theory that land is the source of all wealth would be attracted by a writer who had taken the political standpoint and called land the source of all power.   Montesquieu was certainly acquainted with Harrington.   In one place he coupled him with Plato, Aristotle, Machiavel, and More ;[2]   while in the most famous chapter in all his writings, the chapter on the English Constitution, he gave the following mixed praise.   " Harrington in his ' Oceana ' has also inquired into the utmost degree of liberty to which the constitution of a state may be carried.   But of him indeed it may be said that for want of knowing the nature of real liberty he busied himself in pursuit of an imaginary one ; and that he built Chalcedon, though he had a Byzantium before his eyes." [3]

Whatever attention he had attracted previously, he was at any rate not neglected in the revolutionary

---

[1] " Nouvelles de la République de Lettres," Sept. 1700, p. 243 ff. " Bibliothèque Britannique," July–September 1737. p. 408 ff. Cf. also Dedieu, " Montesquieu et la Tradition politique Anglaise en France," pp. 12 and 62.

[2] " Spirit of the Laws," i. 174.   London 1878.

[3] Ibid. ii. 269.

period. In 1794 the librarian of the Bibliothèque Nationale wrote a short article in the " Moniteur," in which after commending especially the famous petition of July 6th, and criticising the Puritan tendency of Harrington's writings he appealed for a good edition of " Oceana." The article expressed the preference for an edition over a translation. In the following year this appeal was partly answered, for translations of Harrington's " Works " and his " Political Aphorisms " were published.[1] And it was claimed that all that was necessary for the salvation of France was a realisation of Harrington's theories. If institutions were sufficiently good and sufficiently well safeguarded, no Cromwell or Robespierre (it was somewhat early to write Napoleon) could destroy them.

There was one reason in particular, which might make the French sympathetic towards Harrington. The same good fortune or insight which had enabled him to prophesy the independence of America, enabled him to forecast the revolutionary ascendancy of France. " If," he had written, " France, Italy, and Spain were not all sick, all corrupted together, there would be none of them so ; for the sick would not be able to withstand the sound, nor the sound to preserve their health without curing of the sick. The first of these nations (which, if you stay her leisure, will in my mind be France) that recovers the health of antient prudence, shall certainly govern the world."[2] This extraordinary prophecy was soon pointed out. In a letter to the " Moniteur," dated

[1] The " Works " were translated by P. F. Henry in 3 vols. The " Aphorisms " by Aubin.

[2] " Oceana," p. 203. Nevile's more definite prophecy of the Revolution (Plato Redivivus, pp. 140 and 147) should also be compared.

March 13th, 1796, a member of the Conseil des
Anciens quoted it and strongly urged anyone who
took reading seriously, to study an author who had
been misjudged by Montesquieu and but partially
appreciated by Adams.

The motives for turning to a writer like Harrington are intelligible. " Oceana " was the most
important Utopia of the English Rebellion. The
troubles and disputes with which it dealt were similar
to those that were engaging France. The battle
between the single- and double-chamber systems was
as lively in France as it had been in England and
America. The same arguments were used in all
three countries. The respective claims of manhood
suffrage and property qualifications were urged in
exactly the same language.[1] The necessity for
toleration was no less strong because atheists occupied
the scene instead of sectarians. Methods of voting,
methods of election, methods of avoiding concentration of power—these and a thousand other questions were being discussed. France had its socialists
clamouring for an " agrarian law," its communist
chimæras, and its assaults on primogeniture. In
short the great problems of the French Revolution
were very like those of the English Rebellion ; for
politics are independent of nationality, and when
a nation becomes self-conscious there are certain
fundamental questions with which it is bound to
grapple.

[1] I select the following two arguments by way of illustration, each being
extremely similar to Harrington's own arguments for property qualifications.

" The merchant easily sends his fortune abroad ; the capitalist, the banker,
the monied man are cosmopolitan ; the proprietor is the only true citizen ;
he is chained to the soil." " Point de Jour," iii. 488.

" It is obvious that the owners of land or property, without whose consent
no one in the country can either lodge or eat, are its citizens *par excellence*."
Aulard, " French Revolution," iii. 280.

In order to determine the extent to which Harrington was read, it would be necessary to examine much of the pamphlet literature of the Revolution—a task outside the scope of a study like the present. Even if much was read, it would be difficult to decide what to attribute to Harrington's influence and what to the influence of America, Venice, the classics, and other things with which Harrington himself was connected. It is more profitable to concentrate on one figure in the Revolution, the Abbé Sieyès ; for in France it was to him, just as in America it was to Adams, that any real influence on the part of Harrington is due.

Burke has compared Harrington with Sieyès.[1] The comparison is a good one, for their careers offer many parallels. Outside of parties and averse to extremes they both survived a revolution and at the end could boast " J'ai vécu." Each was the most eminent theorist of his time, and as framers of paper constitutions they stand out above other names in history. Their methods were similar. Harrington wrote a political romance ; Sieyès expressed his approval of political romances and himself dictated one. Both thought that in doing so they were bringing a scientific contribution to politics, so that Harrington was compared with Harvey and Sieyès was called by his contemporaries a political Newton.[2] Each was fond of the epigram ; it was the weapon with which Sieyès, as it were, punctuated the French Revolution. Sieyès was a somewhat more practical statesman, and he came into prominence at an earlier stage in the French movement than Harrington in the English. But both achieved their greatest publicity at the end of the revolutions in which they

---

[1] "Works," v. 242. " Letter to a noble lord."
[2] Sainte Beuve, " Causeries du Lundi," v. 155.

took a part, when the building of a Constitution was imperative. The great difference was that Sieyès found the Man who would accept and put into practice his ideas before he made them obsolete. Harrington's ideas, as far as England was concerned, remained on the paper on which they were written.

It was Bonaparte who eventually accepted and put into practice Sieyès' constitutional ideas. But the Abbé had formulated his theories long before, and as occasions had presented themselves made them public. By the end of the year 1789 the absurdity of calling the unrepresentative members of the Third Estate " The National Assembly " was generally realised. They had been elected by obsolete electoral divisions, which antedated the formation of the centralised French state. They could in no way be said to represent the nation. Sieyès with his supreme belief in representative government was the last to tolerate this. He went straight to the root of the question, proposed the abolition of the old divisions, and suggested a new and more scientific system of dividing France, which would make a national assembly possible.

The work was begun at once and France was divided into eighty departments of nearly equal size, which were in their turn divided into districts and cantons. Each department contained six districts, each district nine cantons, each canton ten municipalities. At the same time the whole system of local government was revised and a uniform scheme was adopted. All officials, judicial and executive included, were made elective, and the ballot and rotation, which had been found in some places, were made compulsory.

For ten years Sieyès spasmodically kept his

political views before Paris and stood as the champion of centralisation and the representative system. His position was not an easy one. The departments of his own creation from time to time asserted a considerable degree of independence, and the federalists who noted this with satisfaction could quote the important example of the United States of America. The referendum also had its partisans, and Rousseau's contention that the English people were only sovereign at general elections was widely accepted. But Sieyès remained firm. He believed that representation was the best way of making popular sovereignty genuine. Discussion was to him the great means of ascertaining the general will. In a word France was to be made democratic by the free employment of debate, strong by a scientific centralisation of government, free by a separation of the legislative and executive.

It seems probable that the scheme for dividing France afresh was borrowed directly from Harrington. Contemporaries thought so, and the assertion was made in the "Gazette."[1] The idea at any rate is the same. Harrington's contention was that reform must begin from the bottom and work upwards and outwards, and the redivision of England was the point of departure in all his propositions and the first organic law of Oceana. New wine cannot be put into old bottles. The unequal size of the counties was an attribute and a support of monarchical institutions ; republicanism needs equality even in political divisions. " When the Constituent Assembly decreed the division of the territory into departments, districts, cantons, and communes," wrote a French republican,

[1] Morellet, " Memoirs," i. 415. Quoted by J. H. Clapham, " The Abbé Sieyès," p. 32.

" I cried from the midst of my friends, ' There is the Republic.' " [1]

For ten years it was known that Sieyès had a ready-made Constitution in his head embodying these ideas. In discussing the Constitution of 1795 he had divulged the outlines of his ideal State. He had again insisted on a division of powers to prevent despotism and a centralised government to prevent anarchy, and he had revealed two of his proposals. The first was to reject the ordinary double-chamber system to which the framers of the Constitution had reverted, and to replace it by a scheme which would serve to differentiate powers more closely—Harrington's peculiar system. The second was his famous Constitutional Jury, which (as he explained in the " Moniteur ") was to consist of 108 members, of whom one-third should retire annually and be replaced from those retiring from the two chambers. Their duties were to be threefold. They were to be the guardians of the Constitution and prevent all unconstitutional legislation, like the body proposed in Harrington's petition.[2] They were to revise the Constitution every ten years on proposals made to them by the people. They were to act as a jury of equity. He had submitted these two proposals, but had gone no further. Now, in 1799, when the Man had come upon the scene to found a Utopia, Sieyès was induced to make a full and systematic exposition of his scheme. He refused to put it into writing, but dictated it to his friend and follower Boulay de la Meurthe.

The structure, as anticipated, rested in the first place on the redivision of the country. The system of 1789 was to be retained but larger units called

---

[1] Aulard, "French Revolution," i. 215.   [2] Above, p. 88.

arrondissements were substituted for the 44,000 municipalities. The arrondissement thus became the primary territorial division and the first electoral unit in place of the petty commune. The electoral system on which the scheme was based was somewhat complicated. There were to be three great lists, the list of the arrondissement, the list of the department, and the national list. The first was formed by all the male adults in each arrondissement, who selected by ballot one-tenth of their number as their representatives. These acted as electors of the second list, which was formed by a reduction of their number to one-tenth. These in their turn were electors of the third list, which was formed by a similar decimal reduction. Communal offices were to be filled from the first, departmental from the second, and national from the third list. And to ensure the absolute purity of elections provision was made for a possible disqualification of another tenth from all these lists, so that suspicious names which had passed the tests of the ballot and the indirect election might be expunged. Yet one more precaution was added in the shape of a revival of the old Athenian device, ostracism.

The government was to be divided into legislative, executive, and what Sieyès called "constituent." The legislative bodies were two. The Tribunate was to keep in touch with popular ideas, receive petitions, and initiate measures in response to demand. The Legislative Body was to vote on their proposals without discussion. The executive was to consist of a Grand Elector, his two consuls with their Council of State, and lesser officers nominated by them. The "constituent" was to consist of a College of Conservators enjoying life membership and charged with the duties of selecting the two legislative bodies and the Grand Elector from the national list and generally with watching over the Constitution. Though the legislative bodies were actually two, and had the same duties as the two bodies in " Oceana," no fewer than four had the power to deal with legislation. Proposals came either from the popular source, the Tribunate, or the governmental source, the legally trained Council of State; they were argued by both bodies before the Legislative Body, who recorded their votes in silence; but even their decisions could be vetoed as unconstitutional by the College of Conservators.

Two more features of the plan may be noticed. Firstly, the system of rotation was extended from local to central government, one quarter of the Legislative Body retiring annually and being ineligible for immediate re-election. Secondly, although manhood suffrage was instituted and property qualifications were deliberately rejected, the Grand Elector and the members of the College were to be very highly paid—and to be paid in land.

The parallel between this and " Oceana " is very striking. Departments, districts, arrondissements stand for tribes, hundreds, parishes. Where one-fifth of the whole number of voters were selected in " Oceana " to form the first list, one-tenth were chosen in Sieyès scheme. The two schemes of indirect election differ in detail but are the same in principle. Ballot and rotation appear in both, and in both debating and voting are differentiated. Both, too have their imitations of the Spartan ephorate, " Oceana " its Council of War, Sieyès' scheme its College of Conservators. Finally there is the striking provision in Sieyès' scheme that the highest officials of the country must have large landed property. It is absurd to imagine that every detail of Sieyès' ideal state was borrowed from " Oceana." The ballot, rotation, and indirect election had long been known in France, and Rousseau had already proposed a revival of the Spartan ephorate. But it would be more absurd to attribute nothing to its influence. We know that Sieyès' was a doctrinaire type of mind, we know that he read English political writings, we know that Harrington was sufficiently respected in France to find a translator, and we know that it was believed at the time that Sieyès was imitating him. We may therefore conclude that Sieyès did study and borrow from his own counterpart in the English Rebellion.

The scheme formed the basis of the Constitution of the year 1800, which was introduced by Bonaparte. Bonaparte was no admirer of Sieyès. At the best he was an " idéologue," at the worst " a mediocre intelligence." [1] But some constitution was necessary for a nation in the throes of disorder, and Sieyès' scheme was not without possibilities. Bonaparte therefore accepted it, but mortified Sieyès by insisting on introducing certain modifications into a plan, which had been cherished for years as perfect and therefore unalterable. The changes were not important nor did they affect the Harringtonian features of the Constitution to a serious extent, but they showed the tendency of things. No provisions, however elaborate, could prevent Bonaparte from gradually asserting his personality. His first consulship was soon made perpetual and, before four years had passed, he had assumed the title as well as the powers of Emperor.

For a long time he permitted the weakened Tri-

[1] Thibaudeau, " Bonaparte and the Consulate," p. 136 and xxxviii.

bunate and the Council of State to appoint their
orators to present his proposals before the silent
legislature. The legislative body, unlike those in
Carolina and Pennsylvania, apparently was contented with its mute existence. But Bonaparte
himself could never understand the system of checks
and balances. A speechless assembly appeared silly.
" Three hundred men who never speak a word !
What an absurdity ! " [1] he said on one occasion ;
and on another, " these deaf and dumb legislators in-
vented by Sieyès are simply ridiculous." [2] For some
time he let them be, but in 1804 he gave them the
power of discussing legislative proposals in secret
committee ; and the final attempt to work a lower
chamber on Harrington's principle failed.

Although Harrington's idea of a representative
referendum was thus rejected, another of his theories,
which had been almost entirely disregarded, was
now partly accepted and put into practice. In
1796 Burke had written of the Revolution in the
following strain : " We have not considered as we
ought the dreadful energy of a state, in which the
property has nothing to do with the government.
Reflect, my dear sir, reflect again and again, on a
government, in which the property is in complete
subjection, and where nothing rules but the mind
of desperate men. The conditions of a commonwealth not governed by its property, was a combination of things, which the learned and ingenious
speculator Harrington, who had tossed about society
into all forms, never could imagine to be possible.
We have seen it ; the world has felt it ; and if the
world will shut their eyes to this state of things, they
will feel it more. The rulers there have found their

[1] Thibaudeau, " Bonaparte and the Consulate," p. 45.   [2] *Ibid.* p. 267.

resources in crimes." [1] Burke here diagnosed the cause of much of the confusion with his usual penetrative insight, and France under the Consulate began to realise the truth of his criticism.

As in Carolina and Pennsylvania it was first proposed to form a " house of proprietors " to ensure the representation of property, probably in imitation of the House of Lords. The idea was never accepted, but certain steps were taken to bring the position of property more closely into line with the altered conditions. In the first place property qualifications were instituted for the permanent Electoral Colleges, which Bonaparte had substituted for Sieyès' lists. As Bonaparte himself said, doubtless unconscious of his authority, " we must have men of property in the Electoral Colleges, *because property is the fundamental basis of all political power.*" [2] In the second place the property of the Emigrés was declared national property, open to purchase by supporters of the Republic. In the third place a new nobility was formed of Princes, Counts, Barons, and Knights, to whom lands were assigned outside France with the recommendation to exchange them for lands in France as opportunity offered. Princes were given seats in the powerful Senate, already made more powerful. All four orders were made hereditary for those who could pass down to their heirs a sufficiently large property, and to make this more easy the fourth provision for bringing power and property together —the equal division of property among the children —was modified for them.

That property must rule was a commonplace that may have been taken from the English Whigs or extracted from decadent feudalism. Unlike

---

[1] Burke, " Works," v. 341.   [2] Thibaudeau, p. 251.   The italics are mine.

Adams, Burke, and Hume many were doubtless
unconscious of the first exponent of the idea. But
the French translation of Moyle's essay (1801), which
applied the doctrine in detailed fashion to Roman
history, shows that there were some people in France
who realised its origin. It is at any rate probable
that through whatever channel it had come, this
theory was partly responsible for the shifting of property produced by the Revolution. For this reason
as well as for his influence on the elaborate schemes
of Sieyès and the re-division of the country, which has
survived all the changes of the nineteenth century,
Harrington deserves a place, however small, in the
history of the French Revolution.

Harrington was an interesting man rather than a
great man. Living at an important period in the
history of England, he produced a Utopia written
in language which is generally interesting and sometimes picturesque, in which he embodied theories
that were partly original and partly borrowed from
Continental sources. He proceeded to repeat these
on every possible occasion carrying on a campaign,
which has its modern counterpart in the editor of
the " Spectator's " campaign on behalf of the Referendum. For a time he was a public figure of
some notoriety and one of the originators of the
political clubs and coffee-house politics, for which
London became famous. At the Restoration he
suffered imprisonment and lost his reason in consequence of the ill-treatment which he received.
" Oceana " soon became a classic. Its theories gave
support to the dominance of the landed classes in the

eighteenth century and also played a part in the introduction of the ballot in the nineteenth. In America they received extraordinary attention. The main provisions of "Oceana" were put into practice in Carolina, Pennsylvania, and New Jersey, and in spite of their partial failure they were revived during the Revolution, which they had helped to produce. Through the medium of Sieyès they passed to France, where they met with a similarly modified success.

Harrington's history brings out the affinity between the three revolutions of England, America, and France in a striking manner. It also serves as an illustration of the connection between political theory and practice. His work was of equal value for the way in which it explained the representative system and the way in which it emphasised the economic view of history. In many respects he was far ahead of his time. It took England over two hundred years to realise the value of the ballot, which is now regarded as one of the keystones of democracy. The referendum, which he foreshadowed in his parliamentary system, has never been canvassed seriously until the present day. It was only two years ago that his scheme of rotation was embodied in Lord Lansdowne's proposal for the reform of the House of Lords. Harrington was conscious of the value of his work and yearned for fame. He did not get what he wanted in his lifetime and his name is almost forgotten to-day. But it is now possible after the lapse of time to see him in the correct historical perspective and give him the portion that is his due.

APPENDIX

MOYLE'S ESSAY ON *THE ROMAN COMMONWEALTH*

(See pp. 139 and 143)

THE first part of Moyle's essay on the " Roman Commonwealth " is to be found in manuscript at the Record Office in the Shaftesbury Papers, Bundle 47, No. 4. Its publication in Moyle's collected works has apparently not been noticed, and it has hitherto been accepted as a juvenile work of Locke's. First published in 1726 and republished in 1796 it was a book that was read in America; and in 1801 it was translated into French. Moyle's acceptance of the theory of the balance of property was complete. " It appears," he wrote, " that land is the true center of power, and that the Balance of Dominion changes with the Ballance of Property, as the needle in the compass shifts its points, just as the great Magnet in the earth changes its place. This is an eternal truth, and confirmed by the experience of all ages and governments, and so fully demonstrated by the great Harrington in his ' Oceana ' that 'tis as difficult to find out new arguments for it, as 'tis to resist the cogency of the old ones."

The most interesting feature of the essay is the way in which Roman parallels are employed. In arguing that the republican institutions of Rome were due to the agrarian, the written constitution, the prohibition of the payment of fees and pensions to advocates, the exclusion of the augurs from the comitia tributa, the age qualification for magistracy, the short terms of office, the measures to prevent accumulation of offices, the ballot and other securities against bribery, and finally the provision by which the abolition of monarchy and the institution of the tribunate were made " the fundamental branch of the Constitution," it is obvious that Moyle is thinking primarily of the actual suggestions of the English republicans and is arguing back to Roman parallels.   It is possible that some of the ideas that inspired the English Rebellion were drawn by direct imitation from the classical writers.   But more commonly the classics were searched to provide parallels for modern ideas.   For example, no one would pretend that the proposal to exclude priests and divines from parliament was due to the Roman practice of excluding the augurs from the comitia tributa.   The classics furnished ideas as well as parallels, but in estimating their influence it is well to remember the way in which they were used by men like Moyle.

INDEX

A

Academy, The, 70–1, 72
Adams, John, 186–99, 201, 204, 214
Agreement of the People, 24, 41
American Colonies, Harrington prophesies independence of, 67–8, 187, 203 ; his influence in, 153–200
Anacharsis, 113
Angers, 39
Antidotum Britannicum, 134
Arderne, James, 103
Aristotle, 20, 32, 113, 125, 188, 202
Army, The, in *Oceana*, 60–2
Ashburton, 149
Ashton, Lady, 3 n., 125
Aubrey, John, 7, 88–9, 101, 102, 103, 107, 108, 113, 127, 167
Australian Commonwealth, 179

B

Bacon, 14, 15, 19
Bagshaw, Edward, 103
Balance of Property, 18, 23–36, 79, 81–4, 86, 98, 105, 113, 118–20, 130, 133, 134–5, 140, 144, 146–8 ; in Carolina, 157–9, 160, 161 ; in New Jersey, 164 ; in Pennsylvania, 175–6; in America, 198, 199–200, 212–4, 217–8
Ballot, previous employment of, 37–9 ; in *Oceana*, 46, 50, 59 ; advocated by Shaftesbury, 138 ; and others, 141, 143 ; history of, in England, 149–51 ; in Carolina, 158, 199 ; in New Jersey, 162–3, 199; in Pennsylvania, 168, 174, 177, 180, 183, 199 ; in France, 209, 210
Bamfield, 170, 175
Bank of England, The, 149
Barebones, Praisegod, 88, 123, 125
Barwick, Dr, 93
Baxter, Richard, 45, 113, 114, 116–7
Baynes, Captain, 81–4
Behemoth, 16
Bentham, Jeremy, 150
Berkeley, Lord, 162
Bern, 42
Bernard, 143, 202

Bishops' War, First, 5
Blackstone, 189
Bolingbroke, 143
Bonaparte, Napoleon, 206, 211–3
Bonar's *Philosophy of Political Economy*, 23
Booth, Sir George, 87, 95
Boston Gazette, 107
Boston Public Library, 192, 195
Boulay de la Meurthe, 208
Bray, Captain, 113
Bryce, James, 179
Bunkers Hill, 189
Burke, 205, 212, 214
Burnet, Gilbert, 115, 144
Butler, Samuel, 100, 105

C

Calves' Head Club, The, 101–2
Carisbrooke Castle, 6
Carolina, 155, 157–61, 172, 179, 181, 191, 192, 199, 212, 213
Carteret, Sir George, 124, 125, 160, 162
Carteret, Phillip, 103
Censorship of the Press, 9
Chalmers' *Political Annals*, 163
Charles I., 5–7
Charles II., 107, 111, 122
Checks and Balances, 196, 197, 199, 212
Chillingworth, William, 3
Choate, Rufus, 196
Cicero, 188, 189
Classics, influence of the, 14, 16–7, 21, 26, 30, 32, 35, 49–50, 60, 61, 65, 71, 72–3, 106, 133–4, 187n., 188, 201, 217–8
Claypole, Lady, 10
Coke, Roger, 103
Coleridge, 22, 182
Collins (member of the Rota), 103
Colonies, Harrington's views on, 67–8, 187
Companies, merchant, 37, 39, 41, 154
Connecticut, 39, 195
Constitutional Jury, 208
Cornwall Lewis, 23

219

Trenchard, 145, 186
Turgot, 187, 196
Tyrconnel, Earl of, 102

U

Universities, 60, 69–70
Utilitarians, The, 149
Utopia, 12

V

Vane, Sir Henry, 24, 80, 85, 89, 96, 97, 98, 99, 101, 108, 111
Venice, visited by Harrington, 4, 5, 7 ; Howell's history of, 14 ; *Paruta's History*, 21 ; the ballot at, 37, 39, 139, 171, 174 ; admiration of, in 17th century, 38 ; indirect election at, 40 ; indirect referendum at, 42 ; Church and State at, 59 ; Harrington criticised for imitating, 114, 115
Venner, 103, 123
Vergil, translated by Harrington, 7–8

Vindiciæ contra Tyrannos, 186
Virginia, 191, 192
Virginia Company, 39
Voltaire, 182, 190

W

Walker, Sir Edward, 124
Wallas, Graham, 48n.
Wallingford House, 80, 85
Warren, General, 189
Washington, George, 153, 167, 200
Webster, Noah, 199
Wildman, John, 76, 87, 103, 123, 124, 125
William III., 166, 185
Williams, Roger, 165
Windsor, 6
Winstanley, Gerard, 14, 15, 27–8, 48
Wisbech, 39
Wither, George, 42, 48
Wolfe, 189
Wood, Robert, 103
Wordsworth, 22, 182
Wotton, Sir Henry, 38
Wren, Matthew, 79, 100, 113, 118, 119, 120